Collected Poems

H. L. Mencken
Collected Poems

Edited by S. T. Joshi

Hippocampus Press
New York

Introduction and editorial matter
copyright © 2009 by S. T. Joshi

Published by Hippocampus Press
P.O. Box 641, New York, NY 10156.
www.hippocampuspress.com

This volume has been authorized by the Enoch Pratt Free Library of Baltimore, in accordance with the terms of the will of H. L. Mencken. Photograph of H. L. Mencken by Robert H. Davis published by permission of the Enoch Pratt Free Library, Baltimore, in accordance with the terms of Mr. Mencken's will.

Cover design by Barbara Briggs Silbert.
Hippocampus Press logo designed by Anastasia Damianakos.

All rights reserved.
No part of this work may be reproduced in any form or
by any means without the written permission of the publisher.

First Edition
1 3 5 7 9 8 6 4 2

ISBN: 0-9824296-3-0
ISBN-13: 978-0-9824296-3-1

Contents

Introduction *by S. T. Joshi*	9
To R. K.	15
The Four-Foot Filipino: A Ballad of the Trenches	16
The Tin-Clads	17
Joe and Bobs	19
Auroral	20
One Man Band	21
A Frivolous Rondeau	23
A Few Lines	24
The Roorback and the Canard	25
Chrysanthemum	26
Canzonette	27
[Untitled]	28
An Ante-Christmas Rondeau	29
The Dawn of Love	30
[Untitled]	31
Fidelis ad Urnum	32
[Untitled]	33
A Ballad of Impecuniosity	34
A War Song	35
A Madrigal	36
A Song for Autumn	37
Nocturne	38
An Ode to a "Stein"	39
The Filipino Maiden	40
A Rondeau of Two Hours	42
When the Pipe Goes Out	43
Thanksgiving Day	44
Adlai	45
A Dirge	46
A Bacteriolgal Romance	47
To O. P. K.	48
And Now Comes Congress	49
The Man That Guards the Grub	50
A Ballad of Looking	52
Well Buried	53
The Orf'cer Boy	54

A Paradox	55
Madrigal	56
The Song of the Slapstick	57
An Old, Old Story	58
Love and the Rose	59
The Coming of Winter	60
Outside, Old Year!	61
To Isaackhanmofakhammeddovlet	62
The Boy and the Man	64
The Donation Party	65
To Kruger	68
A Rondeau of Statesmanship	70
In Eating Soup	71
Serenade	72
Im Hinterland	73
The Snow	74
A Ballad of Fierce Fighters	75
The Pantoum of Congress	77
To Mrs. Nation	79
In Vaudeville	80
A Slug of Pessimism	81
An Ode to Nelson A.	82
To G. W.	84
A Sonnet to a Wienerwurst	85
The Ballade of the Rank and File	86
To Wu Ting Fang, Envoy Extraordinary and Minister Plenipotentiary	87
On Phyllis at the Play	89
Theatrical Alphabet	90
April	92
Dawn	93
A Villanelle	94
The Transport Gen'ral Ferguson	95
Faith	97
The Spanish Main	98
The Rondeau of Riches	99
A Ballade of Protest	100
Preliminary Rebuke	101
The Song of the Olden Time	102
The Ballad of Ships in Harbor	103
The Violet	105
September	106

Arabesque	107
The Rhymes of Mistress Dorothy	108
Roundel	110
Within the City Gates	111
Il Penseroso	112
Finis	113
War	115
On Passing the Island of San Salvador	117
Starting for the Play	118
Good-By, Divine Sarah!	120
The Old Trails	121
The Ballade of Cockaigne	122
Song	123
Invocation	124
The Voices	125
Appendix: A Kruger, *by Edmond Rostand*	127
Notes	129
Index of Titles	139
Index of First Lines	143

INTRODUCTION

It is well known that H. L. Mencken's first published book was a volume of poetry, *Ventures into Verse* (1903), issued before his twenty-third birthday. The book contained 39 poems, most of which had been previously published in magazines and newspapers dating from 1899 to 1903. What is not widely known, except to the most devoted Menckenian, is that Mencken published more than 50 more poems both before and after the issuance of *Ventures into Verse*, extending to as late as 1915, or shortly after his assumption of the coeditorship of the *Smart Set*. Mencken may well have blanched at the idea of this body of work being collected in a volume: he had already declared emphatically, in an essay on the publication of *Ventures into Verse*, that "there will never be a second edition";[1] and even when assembling "that embarrassing volume," he was mortified to find "how little critical sense I had in 1902, when it was put together. It includes some imitations of Kipling that must hold a world's record for banality, and some essays in old French forms that are almost as bad, but it also shows a few things that are markedly better."[2]

It is, perhaps, that final grudging remark that partially justifies the publication of this volume. To be sure, we have long ago reached the stage where anything emanating from the pen of Henry Louis Mencken will be of interest to the not inconsiderable band of followers who hang on his every word, and the early writings of any author as important as Mencken deserve our attention for the hints they may offer of the great work to come. In his literary novitiate Mencken was both an ardent writer of poetry—he tells us that as early as 1897 "I resolved solemnly to write at least one poem every day, and for weeks on end I actually did so"[3]—and of short fiction, and both these bodies of work have been unjustly ignored by those who see only the fiery journalist and critic who shaped the culture of 1920s America. But the revelation that Mencken devoted a substantial amount of effort to creative writing such as poetry and fiction should, at a minimum, cause us to re-evaluate some of our assumptions on the kind of writer Mencken was and hoped to be.

Mencken was accurate in saying that the verse of Rudyard Kipling—

---

1. "On Breaking into Type," *Colophon* 1, no. 1 (February 1930): 8. In even this prediction Mencken was wrong, for there was a second edition—a facsimile of the first—that appeared from Smith's Book Store (Baltimore) in 1960.
2. *My Life as Author and Editor* (New York: Alfred A. Knopf, 1993), p. 6.
3. Ibid.

then at the height of his popularity and critical esteem (and, perhaps, notoriety, as witness his ambiguous but controversial poem "The White Man's Burden" [1899])—was a chief model for his verse. The outbreak of the Spanish-American War in 1898—and especially the extension of that war to the Philippines, which metamorphosed from a Spanish colony into an American protectorate only after the U.S. Army harshly suppressed a native rebellion in 1901—allowed Mencken to act as a kind of American Kipling in speaking both of the thrill of battle ("The Tin-Clads") and its pathos ("Joe and Bobs," among several others). Indeed, Mencken's early poetic tribute to Kipling ("To R. K.") was followed up a few years later by the tart "A Ballade of Protest," which urges Kipling to return to the rugged, "masculine" style of his early verse—the verse found, specifically, in *Barrack-Room Ballads* (1892)—and cease concerning himself with social and political issues. The criticism was not entirely fair, perhaps, for, as we shall see, Mencken himself did not eschew these subjects in his own poetry, but the two poems to Kipling do speak strongly of the strong devotion Mencken had developed to the work of his British contemporary.

The "essays in old French forms" that comprise another major section of *Ventures into Verse*, as well as a substantial residuum of his uncollected poetry, point to Mencken's absorption of such poets as Austin Dobson and Algernon Charles Swinburne, then also enjoying high esteem among critics and readers alike. The very precise rules governing the writing of these forms—triolets, rondeaus, villanelles, etc.—proved to be good practice in literary discipline, and a number of them are far from contemptible. Mencken's lifelong devotion to music is evident in the madrigals, serenades, and songs he composed.

The great majority of Mencken's poetry was published in his own columns of humor and miscellany in the *Baltimore Herald*—"Rhyme and Reason," "Knocks and Jollies," and so forth. In this sense Mencken perhaps did not fully exercise the critical acumen he later displayed as editor of the *Smart Set* and *American Mercury*, for the need to fill copy every week, or even twice a week, necessitated his inclusion of poems on very transient topical issues or those whose aesthetic polish was perhaps not of the highest. Nevertheless, a number of entertaining ditties appeared, ranging from the finely Kiplingesque "The Man That Guards the Grub" to the amusing satire "To Mrs. Nation," about the temperance advocate Carry Nation, whose antics Mencken could not have looked upon with approval. His own "An Ode to a 'Stein'" sufficiently indicates his attitude toward the consumption of alcohol.

The need to be topical led Mencken to devote a number of poems to international affairs—not only to the lingering horrors of the Spanish-American War but to the Boer War (1898–1902), a war in which the United States had no direct role except among those (of whom Mencken may have been one) whose anti-British inclinations led them to support the quixotic Boers in their struggle against the mightiest empire on earth. So early as Christmas of 1900 Mencken had attained such esteem as a poet for the *Herald* that he was tasked with the writing of a poem that occupied an entire page of the paper, in very large decorative type with an enormous illustration flanking each of the two stanzas. This work, "The Boy and the Man," is one of his most poignant war verses, and can take its place with the slightly earlier "A War Song" in its unvarnished depiction of the horrors of war.

As mentioned, Mencken did not shy away from politics in his verse writing. One of the most amusing specimens is "One Man Band," published twice prior to the presidential election of 1900 and presenting a succulent lampoon of the Democratic candidate, William Jennings Bryan. For good measure, Mencken also gave a pungent nose-thumbing to Bryan's running-mate, Adlai Stevenson, in the poem "Adlai." Mencken's general cynicism regarding politics and politicians is well displayed in such satires as "And Now Comes Congress," "The Pantoum of Congress," and "The Roorback and the Canard."

Several of Mencken's poems can be valued for their autobiographical sidelights. I have already noted his paean to the beer stein, to which "A Sonnet to a Wienerwurst" can take its fitting place. "On Passing the Island of San Salvador," although nominally about Christopher Columbus, no doubt drew upon Mencken's own Caribbean voyage of 1900, when he spent several months in Jamaica recuperating from overwork. "A Ballade of the Rank and File" speaks in pathetic tones of the burdens of the lowly journalist, while the number of satirical poems looking askance at love, romance, and marriage lay the foundations for Mencken's chosen persona as the unrepentant bachelor.

Some of the most interesting autobiographical poems are those that treat the theatre, for Mencken's work as a theatre critic began as early as 1904, when he reviewed several stage plays and also vaudeville productions for the *Herald*. His enjoyment of the buffoonery of vaudeville is evident in such poems as "The Song of the Slapstick" and "In Vaudeville." As early as 1901, Mencken took aim at the grotesqueries of the stage in the "Theatrical Alphabet," in which a *Herald* cartoonist wrote colored cartoons accompanying the 26 couplets Mencken wrote for every letter of the alphabet. This series, extending over five Sundays, appeared in the comic section of the paper. One of his last poems for the *Herald* is the clever satire "Starting for the Play," telling of the exasperation of a man who waits for his wife to get ready to go out to the theatre. This poem appeared alongside "Good-By, Divine Sarah!," a send-up of the oft-recurring "farewell" tours that Sarah Bernhardt was wont to make; true enough, her tour of 1905 proved not to be her last visit to the United States.

Mencken suggests that the verses he published in the years after his departure from the *Herald* in 1906—especially the several poems that appeared in the *Smart Set* in 1914–15—had been written earlier: ". . . some [poems] that I wrote during the year or two following *Ventures into Verse* knocked about my desk for years, and some of them did not see print until George Jean Nathan and I took over the *Smart Set* in 1914, and found ourselves so short of copy (and money) that I had to throw in large wads of my own rejected MSS., both in prose and verse."[4] True enough, these poems have the same general feel of his earlier work, and their appearance under unusual pseudonyms suggests that Mencken did not hold them in high regard.

It is likely that more poems exist among Mencken's manuscripts, but for the time being this volume of nearly 100 poems can allow for a comprehensive assessment of Mencken the poet—the humorist, the satirist, the war poet, the political lampooner, even the more orthodox poet of love and the seasons. In the end, Mencken concluded that his work in verse was far from wasted, and his own defense of this phase of his writing forms perhaps the greatest justification for gathering it:

> I am convinced that writing verse is the best of all preparations for writing prose. It makes the neophyte look sharply to his words, and improves that sense of rhythm and tone-color—in brief, that sense of music—which is at the bottom of all sound prose, just as it is at the bottom of all sound verse.[5]

—S. T. Joshi

A Note on This Edition

The poems in this volume are arranged chronologically by date of original publication, either in newspapers, magazines, or in *Ventures into Verse*. Those poems that appeared in *Ventures into Verse* for which original newspaper and magazine publication (if any) has not been ascertained are placed at the end of the 1903 sequence. The poems that appeared in *Ventures into Verse* were in some instances slightly revised from their first appearances, and so the book publication has been followed in these instances. In one case—"The Ballad of Ships in Harbor"—a poem from *Ventures into Verse* was later reprinted in the *Smart Set*, and this version appears to embody slight revisions from the book publication, so the *Smart Set* text has been followed here. I have added light commentary on the poems to elucidate obscure historical, literary, political, and other references in the poems.

I am grateful to Vincent Fitzpatrick for his assistance in securing the texts of some of the poems, and to David E. Schultz for his usual skill in the design of this book.

---

4. Ibid., pp. 6–7.
5. Ibid., pp. 5–6.

Collected Poems

To R. K.

Prophet of brawn and bravery!
  Bard of the fighting man!
You have made us kneel to a God of Steel,
  And to fear his church's ban;
You have taught the song that the bullet sings—
The knell and the crowning ode of kings;
  The ne'er denied appeal!

Prophet of brain and handicraft!
  Bard of our grim machines!
You have made us dream of a God of Steam,
  And have shown what his worship means
In the clanking rod and the whirring wheel
A life and a soul your songs reveal,
  And power and might supreme.

Bard of the East and mystery!
  Singer of those who bow
To the earthen clods that they call their gods
  And with god-like fees endow;
You have shown that these heed not the suppliant's plea,
Nor the prayers of the priest and devotee,
  Nor the vestal's futile vow.

Singer, we ask what we cannot learn
  From our wise men and our schools;
Will our offered slain from our gods obtain
  But the old reward of fools?
Will our man-made gods be like their kind?
If we bow to a clod of clay enshrined
  Will we pray our prayers in vain?

THE FOUR-FOOT FILIPINO

A Ballad of the Trenches

We have chased the slick Apachy over desert, plain, and hill,
    We have trailed the sly Osagy through the bresh,
We have follered Ute and Sioux all their blasted country through,
    When their liquor made them get a little fresh;
We have seen our share of fightin', we have stopped our share of lead,
    We have fought all sorts of fighters, great and small,
But the four-foot Filipino, when it comes to doin' harm,
    Is the toughest proposition of them all.

With his baby bow and arrow, and his Maxim rapid-fire—
    For he carries ev'ry kind of arm that's known—
He's uncommonly successful as a plantin'-squad supplier,—
    On the list of dead his handiwork is shown.
There he squats out in the jungle with his weapon in his hand,
    And a dozen brothers waitin' for his place,
Till a message from your rifle makes him slowly understand
    That it's risky business fightin' face to face.

Then he shuffles to a safer place and waits until you come,
    For he knows you'll travel that way by and by,
When across the swamps and rivers with your rifle you have swum
    Why, he pots you 'fore the mud upon you 's dry!
Ain't he quick! Ain't he slick! Ain't he just a dazzlin' brick!
    Though he's nothin' but a Chinaman, they say,
It is like the crack of doom when you hear his rifle click—
    Bet your life the Filipino ain't a jay!

We have seen our share of fightin', we have stopped our share of lead,
    We have fought all kinds of fighters, great and small,
But the four-foot Filipino, when it comes to pilin' dead,
    Is the most successful piler of them all!

THE TIN-CLADS

The small gunboats captured from the Spaniards and facetiously called "tin-clads" by the men of the land forces, are of great value in the offensive operations against the insurgents along the coast.—[MANILLA DISPATCH]

Their draft is a foot and a half,
And a knot and a half is their speed,
   Their bows art as blunt as the stern of a punt
And their boilers are wonders of greed;
   Their rudders are always on strike,
   Their displacement is thirty-two tons,
They are armored with tin—to the dishpan they're kin—
But their Maxims are A number ones,
                    (Ask Aggie!)
Their Maxims are murderous guns!

When from out the towns and villages, and out the jungle, too,
   We have chased the Filipinos on the run,
Toward the river swamps they foot it—towards the swamps we can't go through—
   And we're doubtful if we've lost the fight or won;
Then when all are safe in hiding in the slimy mud and reeds,
   From the river 'cross the swamp we hear a sound;
It's the sputter and the rattle of the automatic feeds
On the tin-protected cruisers—how they pound—
                    (Sweet sound!)
They that save us being losers—Rah! the tin-protected cruisers!
   Hear their rattling Maxims pound, pound, pound!

When the guns have done their work, and the Tagals come our way,
   (I admit they much prefer us to the guns,)
Why, we finish up what's left—ten in every dozen lay
   Dead as Noah, in the swampy pools and runs;
Then the Maxims stop their rattle and we know that midst the reeds,
   Half a hundred Filipinos on the ground
Are a-looking at the sky, with a glassy, sightless eye,
   And the other half—or most of them—are drowned.

'Twas the tin-protected cruisers—How they pound!
(Sweet sound!)
They that saved us being losers—Rah! the tin-protected cruisers!
How their rattling Maxims pound, pound, pound!

Their draft is a foot and a half
And a knot and a half is their speed,
Their bows are as blunt as the stern of a punt,
And their engines art wonders, indeed.
Their rudders are always on strike,
Their bunkers hold two or three tons,
They are armored with tin—to the meat-can they're kin—
But their Maxims are A number ones,
(Ask Aggie!)
Their Maxims are murderous guns;
(Go ask him!)
Their Maxims are Death's younger sons.

JOE AND BOBS

Old Joe Wheeler and that little feller Bobs—
    Neither one of them has anything to say;
If you'd look at them you'd think they'd find it hard to hold their jobs
    When the regimental band begun to play.
Why, their heads don't reach my shoulder and their fists don't seem as big
    As the bag of pipe-tobacco that I wear,
But you'd bet your hat the enemy performs a dizzy jig
    When old Joe or little Bobs goes on a tear!

Old Joe Wheeler and that little feller Bobs—
    Why, a hundred yards away you'd think they're boys,
But by all that's good and holy, they are mighty funny squabs—
    It's in fighting that they find their greatest joys.
Joe would rather fight than eat, and little Bobs is just the same;
    They are soldiers from their helmets to their shoes,
They are quick and cool and wide-awake and sly and bold and game—
    They're the hardest kind of customers to lose!

Old Joe Wheeler and that little feller Bobs—
    Now their fighting days are pretty nearly done;
On their shoulders triple stars show the record of the wars
    That they've fought and, like a fighter, lost or won.
When at last they sheathe their swords for good and find a soldier's grave,
    When they fall before the all-victorious foe,
We will wait for many a year 'fore we find a pair as brave
    As that little feller Bobs and little Joe!

Auroral

      Another day comes journeying with the sun,
The east grows ghastly with the dawning's gleam,
      And e'er the dark has flown and night is done
The alley pavements with their many teem.

      Another day of toil and grief and pain;
Life surely seems not sweet to such as these!
      Yet they live toiling that they may but gain
The right to life and all life's miseries.

ONE MAN BAND

        Air:—"Whistling Rufus." *Baltimore Herald.*

Out in the west, in the land of silver,
    There lives a phonograph man,
Bryan is his name he was baptized Willy,
    Voice like the shriek of a gale.
And He'll never be still next November—
    Then He'll ride a Republican rail.

    Oh! Willie Billy, your trail is hilly,
        You see votes double; you're chalked for trouble,
    Long you'll remember the month November,
        Sweet Billy Bryan, the one man band.

Steve is the man that's to be a vice—Billy—
    That's what the Democrats say;
Wait till the time comes to count the ballots,
    Wait for election day.
Steve keeps still 'cause he knows that talkin'
    Is Windy Bill's long suit:
How'd you like to be Steve when the music's over
    And he starts out to shoot the chute?

Some people call him the Silver Baby,
    Some call him the Phonograph Bill;
Some say his name should be Rag Time Willie,
    Some say the Human Saw Mill,
Others call him Cyclone or Windy Billy,
    Others the Aeolian Grand,
But the best name of all for the wild Nebraskan
    Is Bryan, the one man band.

Bill is the choice of the Middle-of-the-Road men,
    Choice of the Gutter men, too,
Choice of the men on the barb wire fences,
    Choice of the populists, who
Think they should pay taxes in potatoes,
    Choice of the clover seed mob,
Choice of the whole push of daft gazaboes
    Who've glued their glass eyes on a job.

Something'll drop when Mac and Teddy
    Land on "Bill" with a jar,
Something'll drop when there comes November,
    Bill and Ad'll wonder where they are,
Way down deep 'neath a pile of ballots,
    Mashed by a mountain of votes,
They'll never get out unless they hire
    For the rescue, an army of goats.

Oh! Willy Billy, your path is hilly,
    You're seeing double, you're booked for trouble;
Long you'll remember, the month November,
    Wild Windy Willy, the one man band.

A Frivolous Rondeau

> "I co'd reherse
> A lyric verse."—*The Hesperides*.

A lyric verse I'll make for you,
Fair damsel that the many woo,
    'Twill be a sonnet on your fan—
    That aid to love from quaint Japan—
And "true" will rhyme with "eyes of blue."

Ah! me, if you but only knew
The toil of setting out to hew
    From words—as I shall try to do—
        A lyric verse.

Fleet metric ghosts I must pursue,
And dim rhyme apparitions, too—
    But yet, 'tis joyfully I scan,
    And reckon rhymes and think and plan
For there's no cheaper present than
        A lyric verse.

A Few Lines

Few roses like your cheeks are red,
    Few lilies like your brow are fair;
Few vassals like your slave are led,
Few roses like your cheeks are red,
Few dangers like your frown I dread;
    Few rubies to your lips compare,
Few roses like your cheeks are red,
    Few lilies like your brow are fair.

The Roorback and the Canard

Now comes the roorback
Hustling down the pike
Of politics, with vigor he
Doth hike,
For much he fears
He may arrive too late
To help the prophets to prog-
Nosticate;
It's up to him,
King knocker of them all,
To seek the short and tender ribs
And small
Of those who stand
Within
The calcium's glare;
And there—upon the ribs—
Bring down his fists,
Full forcibly,
Endangering his wrists, that they, or them,
The owners of the ribs,
May suffer,
And with the roorback comes the gay
Canard,
As yet unnailed—
His facial muscles hard as adamant—
Oh! what a pair they are!
It is their aim in life to rude-
Ly jar
Such statesmen as are not
Already jarred.
I'm glad to say I'm not a nominee,
And that I think they will not bother me.

CHRYSANTHEMUM

Now when we mourn the rose and mignonette
    And see the flowers of summer fade and die,
You come, sweet comforter, by storms beset,
    And for our pleasure winter's blows defy.

CANZONETTE

In May they met, in bonnie May,
    Fit time for love and wooing,
When hearts are light and earth is gay;
    They met in May, in bonnie May.

They parted when December's chill
    To earth and hearts brought sorrow;
When flowers were gone and warblers still—
    They parted in December's chill.

Now he is glad the dreams of May
    Must go when comes December;
And she hopes that another May
    Will drive the wint'ry gloom away.

[Untitled]

"Laugh while you can," the poet said;
    He must have been quite ignorant
To think we mortals here below
    Can laugh at any time we can't.

An Ante-Christmas Rondeau

> "'Tis a sad story, mates."—*Marie Corelli.*

It's up to me—the winds are chill
And snow clouds drift from o'er the hill,
    At dawn the rime is on the grass,
    At five o'clock we light the gas,
And long gone is the daffodil.

Jack Frost draws flowers upon the glass
    And blasts the growing ones—alas!
Whene'er he comes to scar and kill,
             It's up to me.

    I run not in the croaker class,
    But when I see the autumn pass,
Of crushing woes I have my fill—
To buy a Christmas gift for Jill
    A horde of gold I must amass—
             It's up to me.

The Dawn of Love

In golden mists the day comes gloriously
    From out the gardens of the dreaming east;
With pomp of power the sun victoriously
    Flings forth his light, from night's black bonds releas't.

In golden mists the boy god airily
    Oft' blinds those whom his arrows would not harm;
The world now views love mercenarily
    And shekels, 'stead of hearts, are Cupid's charm.

[UNTITLED]

Count him for lucky whom all women scorn;
    If one should wed him wherein lie his gains?
The rose must fade and wither, but the thorn
    Remains.

Fidelis ad Urnum

Although you scorn me, I'll forget you not—
    Your face and form will haunt my dreams for aye;
Though in the sweet, sad years kind time may blot
    All other recollection, you alway
    Will in my memory stay!

Though earth grow topsy-turvey and the sight
    Of fishes grazing and of cows in trees
Grow common, and the sun illume the night
    And moon the day, and farmers plow the seas,
    You'll haunt my fantasies!

Although mine eyes be dimmed by age's breath,
    Still, in my mind, your image will not fade;
If you should die, I'll calmly wait for death,
    And then, unless my borrowed five is paid,
    I'll dun your shade!

[Untitled]

Sweethearts often quarrel upon
The slightest provocation,
    Because they love
        The pleasure of
The reconciliation.

A Ballad of Impecuniosity

"All the World's a Graft."—Tommy Hawk.

When you've spent your bottom dollar
   And your credit's taken wings,
And the smell of ham and cabbage makes you weep;
   When your watch is ticking gaily
   'Mid the heap of other things
That your Uncle's kindly promised you to keep;
   When your tank of hope is empty,
   And your smile balloon has "bust,"
And your final cup of pleasure has been quaffed,
   Then's the time to show your manhood—
   Do not wallow in the dust!
But arise—and like a man—set out to graft!

   Fate may jar your solar plexus,
   Luck may drop you by the board,
Woes may roost, like hungry vultures, on your trail;
   You may hang above a chasm
   By a mighty slender cord
And be blown about in dark misfortune's gale;
   But although you're up against it
   And the waves are o'er your head,
Do not weep!—it's easy enough to make a raft
   Of your luckier fellow-beings—
   Let them labor in your stead
While you watch them—that's the way to work a graft!

A War Song

The wounded bird to its blasted nest,
    (Sing ho! for the joys of war!)
When the sun of its life veers o'er to the West,
    (Sing ho! for the war, for the war!)
The wounded fox to its cave in the hill,
And the blood-dyed wolf to the snow-waste chill,
And the mangled elk to the wild-wood rill,
    (Sing ho! for the price of war!)

The nest-queen harks to her master's hurts,
    (Sing ho! for the wounds of war!)
And the she-fox busies with woodland worts,
    (Sing ho! for the end of war!)
The she-wolf staunches the warm red flood,
And the doe is besmeared with the spurting blood,
For 'tis ever the weak that must help the strong,
Though they have no part in the triumph song,
And their glory is brief as their work is long—
    (Sing ho! for the saints of war!)

A Madrigal

How can I choose but love you,
    Maid of the witching smile?
Your eyes are as blue as the skies above you;
How can I choose but love you, love you,
    You and your witching smile?
For the red of your lips is the red of the rose,
And the white of your brows is the white of the snows,
And the gold of your hair is the splendor that glows,
    When the sun gilds the east at morn.
And the blue of your eyes
Is the blue of the skies
    Of an orient day new-born;
And your smile has a charm that is balm to the soul,
And your pa has a bar'l and a many-plunk roll,
    So how can I choose but love you, love you,
Love you, love you, love you?

A Song for Autumn

Oh, the frost is on the pun'kin
    And the mud is on the pike,
And the hick'ry logs are blazin'
    And the tramps are on the hike;
    For the sky's a-gettin' gray
    And the flowers are gone away,
And I scent the snow a-hangin' in the air, air, air;
    It's a-comin' down today
    And I know it's going to lay
'Cause the weather-man's a-prophecyin' "Fair."

Oh, the crows are flyin' s'uth'ard,
    And the hawks are flyin' high,
And the turkey gobbler's ready
    For to help the pun'kin pie
    Make us wish Thanksgivin' Day
    Had a couple weeks to stay.
Oh, I scent the snow a-whirlin' through the air, air, air;
    See the sky a-gettin' gray—
    It's a-comin' down today
'Cause the weather-man's a-prophecyin' "Fair."

Nocturne

How like a warrior on the battlefield
    The city sleeps, with brain awake, and eyes
    That know no closing. Ere the first star dies
It rises from its slumber, and with shield
    In hand, full ready for the fray,
    Goes forth to meet the day.

An Ode to a "Stein"

I.

    O, fount of joy!
    'Tis in thy foamy depths
That all that makes life pleasant doth abide;
    In every drop
    Of amber that thou hold'st
There dwelleth seas of ecstasy beside
Which all the other joys of life are vain.

II.

Wine, women, song!—these be the one and twain
    Of whose delights each hungry bard hath sung
Since the fair moon from Heaven's vault first hung:
    And yet, they are but echoes dim of thee.

III.

Cut women out—their smile is but the key
    To preying woes—and drop song by the board—
What glee is found within a minor chord?
    Then change the wine to foaming malt!

IV.

I would that I could drown myself in thee!

The Filipino Maiden

Her father we've chased in the jungle,
And her brother is full of our lead;
    Her uncles and cousins
    In yellow half-dozens
We've tried to induce to be dead;
    And while we have shot at their shadows,
They've done the same favor for us—
    But, by George, she's so sweet
    That we'd rather be beat
Than to have her mixed up in the fuss.

Oh! isn't her blush like the roses?
And aren't her eyes like the stars?
    And whenever she smiles
    Don't you think you are miles
From the rattle and roar of the wars?
    Would you take the three stars of a general
If she'd say "Leave the stars and take me?"
    Oh! we've stolen sweet kisses from thousands of misses,
But hers are the sweetest that be.

Her name may be Ahlo or Nina,
Or Zanez or Lalamaloo;
    She may smoke the cigars
    Of the chino bazars,
And prefer black maduros to you;
    She may speak a wild six-cornered lingo,
And say that your Spanish is queer,
    But you'll never mind this
    When she gives you a kiss
And calls you her "zolshier poy dear."

Oh! isn't her blush like the roses?
And aren't her eyes like the stars?
    And whenever she smiles
    Don't you think you are miles
From the rattle and roar of the wars?
    Would you take the three stars of a general
If she'd say "Leave the stars and take me?"
    Oh! I've stolen sweet kisses from thousands of misses,
But her's are the sweetest for me!

A Rondeau of Two Hours

> "It's a cinch."—*Plato.*

From four to six milady fair
Is chic and sweet and debonair,
    For then it is, with smiles and tea,
    She fills the chappy mob with glee
(The jays but come to drink and stare).

    A rose is nestled in her hair,
    Like Cupid lurking in his lair—
Few of the jays remain heart free
    From four to six.

    Oh let them come—I would not care
    If all the men on earth were there;
For when they go she smiles on me,
And, just because she loves me, she
    Makes all the ringers take their share
    From four to six.

When the Pipe Goes Out

A maiden's heart,
    And sighs profuse,
A father's foot,
    And—what's the use?

Thanksgiving Day

    Let us give thanks,
    Because—
The men that owe us five don't owe us ten,
The girls we loved have married other men;
    Let us give thanks,
    For why?—
The trains we missed were telescoped and wrecked,
The books we didn't buy were dialect;
    Let us give thanks,
    Because—
The grafts we haven't worked will never pay,
The days we laid abed were dark and gray,
The things we haven't said we didn't say,
    Let us give thanks
    Upon
    Thanksgiving Day.

Adlai

    What's become of Adlai?
    Where's he gone and went?
Seems to me his smilin' face has disappeared from view.
    Back to hoe the cabbages
    Willy Bill was sent—
But what's become of Adlai, the warrior bold and true?

    What's become of Adlai?
    The Hoosier's favorite son,
Hero of the beaten ones, leader of the slain;
    What's become of little Ad?
    What's he gone and done?
Bet he caught his death o' cold standin' in the rain!

    What's become of Adlai?
    Where, oh, where's he at?
Make a search among the morgues; con the list of dead.
    What's become of ——, what's the use?
    There he's layin' flat
Layin' flat upon his back, separate from his head.

A Dirge

     Mum is the man of words,
     Silent the loud Nebraskan,
Dumb is the clarion voice that erstwhile pealed like a bell;
     Cold is the fevered brow,
     As the ears of a chilled Alaskan,
And closed is the muscular mouth that one time gaped like a well.

     Still is the atmosphere
     That the strong lungs agitated,
Dead is the hurtling breeze that switched from the Coast to Maine,
     And dead is W. J. Bryan,
     And to stay dead is he slated
'Till the Salt Creek stern-wheel steamer comes out of the woods again.

A Bacteriologal Romance

A youthful bacilla, an amorous blade,
    Once loved a fair microbe devoutly,
So to her with zest his addresses he paid,
    Protesting his love for her stoutly:
"Ah, no," said the fair one. "It never can be,
  Though you perish of love you will never wed me."
"Alas!" said the am'rous bacilla, "oh, why
  Do you turn me down thusly? Relent, or I'll die!"
"Ah, no!" said the fair one. "It never can be!
  I'm a microbe of gout, and it's fate's sad decree
  That I marry you not, though your heart sigh, 'Alas!'
  A bacilla of measles is not in my class!"

To O. P. K.

      Oom Paul Kruger,
You're a patriot from the top
    Of your headpiece to the bottom of your heels,
When the bloody Britons soldered up the shutters on your shop,
    Why, you loaded up your treasury on wheels.

      O. P. Kruger,
You're a terror in a fuss,
    (Say a Cromwell and a Caesar rolled in one),
You had no desire to loiter in a white sarcophagus
    While the world yet held gazaboes to be done.

      Oom P. Kruger,
Look! my hat is in my hand!
    Slipp'ry Dick is but a mark compared to you;
You have left a few piasters in the Anti-Razor Land
    For to take them all was more than you could do.

      O. Paul Kruger,
You're the hero of the hour,
    And upon your sloping brow are fortune's bays,
O'er the gilded, glinting thaler you have mesmeritic power—
    And you've shown the world that patriotism pays.

AND NOW COMES CONGRESS

And now comes Congress,
Once again to hold
The boards for many
Melancholy moons;
To scrap and knock and croak
And moan and grab
And speechify and please the
Galleries,
And wield the leg-
Islative slap-stick vigorously,
And toot the slide trombone
Of politics,
And hustle after joblets for the
Gang,
And wave the bloody shirt
And starry flag,
And weep and cuss
And spiel and puff hot air,
And throw gay cons
And work seductive grafts,
And pluck the plums
And angle for the fat
And juicy jobs and keep
A deathlike hold
Upon the wagon which
Conveys the band.
Oh! now comes Congress—
It is up to it,
Or them,
To earn the money paid by Uncle Sam,
And pass some other things
Beside
The lie.

The Man That Guards the Grub

If you take a certain view
    (As you're very apt to do),
You will think a colonel's place is rather high,
    And a general's shoulder straps,
    With their triple stars, perhaps,
May be dazzling to your unobservant eye;
    But before you've served a day
    Where a soldier earns his pay
Learning how to shoot and starve and dodge and crawl,
    From experience you'll extract
    The surprising little fact
That the commisary-sergeant tops them all.

He's the man that guards the grub,
Ow, the grub, grub, grub;
And the general in command is his sub, sub, sub!
    On his boxes and his mules,
    Like a king he sits and rules,
He's a roarin' Beelzebub,
Guardin' grub, grub, grub!

    If you want a pinch of flour,
    You must wait a Spanish hour
Till he's made his mind to turn his head your way,
    Then he'll hem and haw and frown
    And proceed to turn you down
In the most unpleasant manner that he may;
    He's a second bloody Czar
    And he makes you think that war
Is a good deal worse than Sherman ever knew,
    He's the army autocrat,
    (And there's little jest in that),
But at times he's mighty good to me and you!
He's the man that guards the grub,

Ow, the grub, grub, grub;
And the general in command is his sub, sub, sub;
    On his boxes and his mules.
    Like a king he sits and rules,
He's a tyrant Beelzebub,
Guardin' grub!

A Ballad of Looking

He looked into her eyes, and there he saw
    No trace of that bright gleam which poets say
    Comes from the faery orb of love's sweet day,
No blushing coyness causes her to withdraw
Her gaze from his. He looked and yet he knew
    No joy, no whirling numbness of the brain,
    No quickening heart-beat. Then he looked again,
And once again, unblushing, she looked too.

He looked into her eyes—with interest he
    Stared at them through a magnifying prism.
    For he was but an oculist, and she
Was being treated for astigmatism.

Well Buried

Ten thousand fathoms deep
Beneath the sea
Of dank oblivion, way down
In the mud
Of used-to-was-iness, way,
Way below
A mountain made of loud
Silurian eggs;
Strapped, corked and sealed and sewed
Up in a sack
And nailed up in a keg
And smoothly tarred
And coated with a feathery
Overcoat;
Deep down among the blind fish and
The worms
And slimy minnows, in the
Sloppy bog;
Far, far below the ken of mor-
Tal man—
There roosts Web Davis, tearful,
Gurgling Web;
And 'round him float the hundred
Thousand plunks
Which op'ed the floor gates of his eloquence
And op'ed the mud gates
On his knotty head.

The Orf'cer Boy

> "He was a gran' bhoy!"—*Mulvaney*.

Now 'e aren't got no whiskers
  An' 'e's only five foot 'igh,
(All the same 'e is a' orf'cer hof the Queen!)
  Oh, 'is voice is like a loidy's
  An' 'e's so polite an' shy!
(All the same 'e serves 'Er Majesty the Queen!)
  It is only 'bout a year ago 'e left 'is mother's knee,
  It is only 'bout a month ago 'e come acrost the sea,
  It is only 'bout a week that 'e 'as been a-leadin' me.
(That's the way 'e serves 'Er Majesty the Queen!)

'E is such a little chappie,
  Bein' only five foot 'igh,
That you'd wonder how 'is likes could serve the Queen;
You would think that when 'e 'eard the guns
  'E'd just set down an' cry—
A-forgettin' ev'rythink about the Queen;
  But by all that's good an' holy, you'd be extraord'ny wrong,
  'Cos 'e doesn't like no singin' 'arf as good 's the Gatlin's song,
  An' 'e fights as though 'e'd been a-fightin' twenty times as long
As any other man that serves the Queen!

If you'd seen him when we got to where
  The Modder's deep an' wet,
You'd a-knowed 'e was a' orf'cer hof the Queen!
There's a dozen of the enemy
  That ain't forgot 'im yet—
For 'e run 'is sword clean through 'em for the Queen!
  Oh, 'e aren't much on whiskers an' 'e aren't much on 'eight,
  An' a year or two ago 'e was a-learnin' for to write,
  But you bet your soldier's shillin' 'e's the devil in a fight—
An' 'ed die to serve 'Er Majesty the Queen!

A Paradox

Dan Cupyd drewe hys lyttle bowe,
    And strayght ye arrowe from it flewe,
Although its course was rather lowe,
    I thought 'twould pass above my heade—
In stature I am shorte, you knowe.

But soone upon my breast a stayne
    Of blood appeared, and showed ye marke
Whereat ye boy god tooke hys aime;
    I staggered, groaned and then—I smyled!
Egad! it was a pleasante payne!

Madrigal

    Ah! what were all the running brooks
From ocean-side to ocean-side,
    And what were all the chattering wrens
That wake the wood with song,
    And what were all the roses red
In all the flowery meadows wide,
    And what were all the fairy clouds
That 'cross the heavens throng—
        And what were all the joys that bide
            In meadow, wood and down,
        To me, if I were at your side
            Within the joyless town?

The Song of the Slapstick

Why is a hen? (Kerflop!) Haw, haw!
    Toot, goes the slide trombone;
Why is a hen? (And a swat in the jaw!)
    And the ushers laugh alone.
Why is a— (Bang!) —is a— (Biff!) Ho, ho!
    Boom! goes the sad French horn;
Why is a hen? (Kerflop!) Do you know?—
    And the paid admissions mourn!

Vhy iss a hen? Yes? No? (Kerflop?)
    Bang! goes the man at the drum;
Vhy iss a hen? (And a knock at the top!)
    And the press agent's stricken dumb;
Vhy iss a— (Thud!) —iss a— (Flop!) —iss a hen?
    Hark! how the supers laugh!
Vhy iss a— (Bing! Bang! Boom!) —and then
    The slapstick's bust in half!

        (Curtain)

An Old, Old Story

Same old Christmas,
    Same old toys,
Same old candies,
    Same small boys.
Same old fruit cake,
    Same old pain,
Same old nuts, and
    List of slain.

LOVE AND THE ROSE

The thorn lives but to shield the rose;
    Coquetry may but shelter love!
(This consolation Hope bestows).
The thorn lives but to shield the rose;
Though blood from many a thorn wound flows
    I'll pluck the rose that blows above—
The thorn lives but to shield the rose,
    Coquetry may but shelter love!

Love me more or not at all,
    Half a rose is less than none;
Hear the wretch you hold in thrall!
Love me more or not at all!
Dilletante love will pall,
    I would have you wholly won;—
Love me more or not at all;
    Half a rose is less than none!

The Coming of Winter

A chill, damp west wind and a heavy sky,
    With clouds that merge in one gray, darkling sea,
The last red leaves of autumn flutter by,
    Wrest from the dead twigs of the street-side tree;
And then there comes an eddying cloud of white,
    First dim, then blotting everything below;
Up to the eaves the sparrows haste in flight—
    And thus upon the town descends the snow.

Outside, Old Year!

    Outside, old year!
        It's up to you to slide.
And few will be your mourners when you go, when you go.
    So long, old year!
        It's up to you to glide—
A pilgrim lost and frozen in the snow, in the snow.
        Twelve months ago a bouncing boy,
            Today the seventh age;
You've had your little chance to speak in public on the stage.
You've had your little chance to strut—
        A mighty personage;
You've had your little chance to claim
        A century's heritage;
And now you're going back to stay
        Forever in your cage.
        Outside, old year!
            You're on the steep tobog;
        So long, old year!
            You're in the sloppy bog!

    Outside, old year!
        We're glad to see you go,
(If only you could help us by departing from our midst!)
        Outside, old year!
        Go wallow in the snow!
(I'm sorry there's no other word that terminates in "idst"!)
        If all our woes could fly with you,
        And all our debts could die with you,
        And troubles say good-bye with you,
            We'd like you rather more;
        But, anyhow, we say to you,
        The while we show the way to you:
        Outside, old year!
            Egad! you were a bore!

To Isaackhanmofakhammeddovlet

Gen. Isaac Khan Mofakhammed Dovlet has been appointed Persian minister to the United States to succeed Gen. Hadji Hassan Gouli Khan Mahomet El Vessari.—Press Dispatch.

Welcome! Isaac!
The latchstring's hanging out,
And we're mighty glad
To say
"We gates"
To you!
The moment that we heard
The news
We loosed a joyous shout,
To wit:
"Oh! Ike, et cetra, how d'y do?"
Come in, Dovlet
And make yourself at home,
We hope you'll like
Your job so well
You'll never yearn to roam,
Or jump a freight for Canada,
Or brave the ocean foam!
Hello, Mofak!
Likewise Fakhammed Ike!
Likewise Fakhammed
Dovlet Isaac Khan!
By George you are
The rarest bird
That's yet come down the pike,
And there's many a
Name about you
That we think
We'll learn to like,
Isaac Khan!
Khan, Khan!

Isaac Khan!
So here's to you,
General Isaac
Dovlet
Mofakhammed
Khan,
Proud successor to the
Other gilded Khan!
General
Hadji Hassan
Vessari
El
Mahomet
Gouli
Khan!
Such a Khan!

The Boy and the Man

(A Christmas Ballad)

  Christmas Eve when the world's before
And the burden of life is a dim unknown
  Christmas!—Snow and the north wind's roar
And the ride of Saint Nick in the night alone,
  With his sleigh piled high and his reindeers shy
  And a smile for the world in his twinkling eye.
Christmas Eve!—and to bed by dark;
Christmas Morn! and awake with the lark;
  Then ho! for the beat of the happy heart,
  For the sad stuffed horse in the small tin cart,
For the glass eyed doll that says, "Mar Mar!"
For the swift red sled and the lead hussar,
  And the stockings that hang by the fireplace—Ho!
  For the joys that came with the Christmas snow!

  Christmas Eve!—and the boy is a man.
And the place for a man is the firing line;
  Christmas Morn!—and the fight began
Ere the stars had paled in the faint dawn-shine;
  And the Tagals broke as the rifles spoke
  And the sunlight burst through the heavy smoke.
Christmas Eve!—and a storm of lead;
Christmas Morn!—and a hundred dead;
  So ho! for the crack of the foeman's gun,
  And ho! for the fight that the hundred won;
And ho! for the boy of the years gone by
Who waited at home for the snow to fly,
  And welcome Saint Nick and the lead hussar—
  Sing ho! he is dead in the war, in the war!

The Donation Party

(A Christmas Cantata)

THE CHARACTERS
The Pastor.
The President of the Y. P. S. C. E.
The President of the King's Daughters.
The President of the Helping Hand Society.
The President of the Busy Bees.
The President of the Willing Workers' Mission Band.
The Pastor's wife.
A cynic.
An elder.
Members of the aforesaid organizations, villagers, servants, deacons, &c.

THE SCENE:
The pastor's parlor.

THE TIME:
Christmas Eve.
(The pastor is discovered sitting in his parlor.)

The Pastor (solus):
    An ecclesiastic's lot,
        Like the melancholy copper's,
    Is distinctly not as happy as it's drawn;
    And the laymen little wot
        How the ante-Christmas shoppers—
(Bell rings.)
    Ha! the annual slipper carnival is on!
(Enter the bunch.)
    What is this? Well, I declare!
        Goodness me! how you surprise me!
    Who'd a thought I'd have this expected joy?
Cynic (aside):
    —Awful joy!

The Pastor:
> Shed your beavers! Have a chair!
> > Why, your kindness fairly shies me!
> I was lucky when I entered your employ.

Cynic (aside):
> —Soft employ!

An Elder:
> It gives me unbounded pleasure to present to you, on behalf of the—

Chorus of Villagers:
> See the Matterhorn of slippers!

President of the Y. P. S. C. E.:
> > In the yard;

Chorus:
> Festive blue and purple slippers—

President of the King's Daughters:
> > Soft and hard;

Chorus:
> Green and pink and yellow slippers!

President of the Helping Hand Society:
> > On a pile;

Chorus:
> Wild and woolly gilded slippers,
> Passing fierce vermillion slippers—

Cynic:
> See him smile!

The Pastor:
> Friends, I thank you for the slippers,
> > Large and small;

Members and Villagers:
> Oh! he thanks us for the slippers,
> > One and all;

Pastor's Wife:
> It was kind to bring him slippers.

Deacons:
> We were kind to think of slippers—

Cynic (aside):
                  Awful kind!
President of the Busy Bees:
        He who wears them's necesarily—
President of the Willing Workers' Mission Band:
           Refined;
Pastor:
        So I thank you for the slippers,
Pastor's Wife:
        For the blue and purple slippers,
Deacons:
        And the gay vermillion slippers,
Elder:
        And the woolly gilded slippers,
Chorus of Members:
        Olive slippers; yellow slippers;
Full Chorus:
        Slippers, slippers, slippers, slippers;
Cynic:
        Varied slippers;
Full Chorus:
        As he thanks us for the slippers,
            Let us go.   (Exit.)

                (Curtain.)

To Kruger

Girt up in state the kings await
      The sound of your knock at the door—
And how will you conquer their hearts with words?
      And what if they smite you sore?

Belike you should hie to the land of pipes
      And Bibles and strong-limbed sons,
Where the tulips have chosen a lily their queen,
      And the blood of your own breed runs.

Belike it may fall that the lily's call
      Shall open the gates of the kings;
And strong with the strength of the pure and the weak,
      She may quell their murmurings.

Belike that the King with the Waxed Moustache,
      Who frowns when you seek him alone,
May clasp your hand with a brother's clasp
      When she swears that your blood is her own!

But alack and alas! if the lily's smile
      Be naught but a gleam of tears;
And alas and alack! If your way lead back
      Through the mist of the hopeless years!

For the tears of a queen, though they gleam as pearls,
      Are dross in the treasure store:
You have bled too oft' by the arrows of churls
      To be wounded enow yet more.

You have known the smart of a heavy heart,
      And a friend that spurned your hand—
And alackaday! If you go your way,
      Hope-dead, to your war-torn land!

Nor ever give heed to the faithless cheers
  Of the mob that would steal your hours,
And let not the kings pay their debt with tears
  And a handful of withering flowers.

The children flock to your carriage-side,
  With silk-tied blossoms rare,—
"Not to France," say you bold, "have I bowed my pride
  For ribbon-writ oaths of air!"

And then, when the crowd gives cheer for cheer,
  Go close your casement down,
For Kruger, man,—if you're half a man—
  You will not be the street boys' clown!

A Rondeau of Statesmanship

In politics it's funny how
A man may tell you one thing now
    And say tomorrow that he meant
    To voice a different sentiment
And vow a very different vow.

The writ and spoken laws allow
Each individual to endow
    His words with underground intent
      In politics.

Thus he who leads in verbal prow-
Ness sports the laurel on his brow—
    So if you wish to represent
    The acme of the eminent,
Learning lying ere you make your bow
      In politics.

In Eating Soup

In eating soup, it's always well
To make an effort to excel
      The unregenerate who sop
      With bread the last surviving drop
As if to them but one befell.

And if it burn you do not yell,
Or stamp or storm or say "Oh!—well!"—
      From social grandeur you may flop
        In eating soup.

And if the appetizing smell
Upon you cast a witch's spell,
      To drain your plate pray do not stop,
      And please, I pray you, do not slop!
A gurgling sound's a social knell
        In eating soup.

Serenade

The stars in the heavens shine down ev'ry night,
    The moon with precision arisen each eve;
But at times inky clouds with malevolent spite,
    Hide both, and their splendor we do not perceive:
Like stars and moon, sweet, my love burns with a flame,
    Unfailing, unchanging, unaltered by years;
Though fell circumstances full oft stop the game,
    When possible, nightly your Clarence appears
        And twangs his guitar,
        And bangs his guitar,
    Until the soft music his lady love hears;
        And bangs his guitar,
        And twangs his guitar,
    Until at her window at last she appears!

I wait, love, I wait, in an uncertain state,
    (Perhaps she's entranced by my sweet serenade!)
Haste, sweet, dawn is nigh, and the hou-er is late,
    And the rising sun soon will these precincts invade;
Smile on me but once, and I'll straightway depart,
    Ecstatic, to live for a day on that smile,
Arise, love, arise, you are breaking my heart,
    And my lungs 'll give out in a very short while.
        I bang my guitar,
        And twang my guitar,—
    Look down and but smile, and I'll satisfied go!
        And take my guitar
        To a region afar—
And take my guitar away!
        (She appears at the window.)

Im Hinterland

(Note—"Hinterland" is a Dutch word signifying the back country, the rural sections, the land far from the coast. It is pronounced nearly, "hin-ter-lont." "Im" is Dutch for in.)

    Im hinterland, im hinterland,
Where roosters crow and porkers grunt,
And cows engage the toothsome cud,
And carrots bloom and turnips bud,
And ways are rough and speech is blunt,
    Im hinterland, im hinterland,
But let a man with fairish front
Set out to do a three-card stunt,
    Im hinterland, im hinterland,
And plenteous coin will flow his way,
For every corruscated jay—
    Im hinterland, im hinterland—
Will buck the game and gladly pay
For opportunity to play
His luck ag'in a certaintay—
    Im hinterland, im hinterland;
And that's the way they are today,
And that's the way they'll be for aye—
You cannot civilize a jay
Or from his belfry pluck the hay,
Alas, alack, alackaday!—
    Im hinterland, im hinterland!

The Snow

A song of birds adown a mine's dark galleries,
    A scent of roses 'mid a waste of moor and fen,
A gush of sparkling waters from the desert sands,—
    So comes the snow upon the town, an alien.

A Ballad of Fierce Fighters

> Gen. Isaac Khan Mafakhammed Davlet, the new Persian minister at Washington, in his own country bears quite a reputation as a Nimrod, particularly in the matter of tigers. He is said to have slain more of those beasts than any other sportsman in Persia.—News Item.

Teddy and Ike are a fearsome pair
    (Powder and shot and a sea of blood),
Stalking the prey to its mountain lair,
Speedy its lope and erect its hair,
Weepful its visage with blank despair
    (Powder and shot and a ruby flood).

Teddy is armed with his snickersnee
    (Powder and shot and a dismal moan),
Isaac is arsenaled cap-a-pie
And the smile that he wears is a smile of glee,
For the hope of his heart is a massacree
    (Powder and shot and a grisly groan).

Teddy has dropped to a tiger's trail
    (Powder and shot and a piercing scream),
He has grabbed the beast by its bushy tail,
And Ike has arrived in his coat of mail,
And the quivering beast is ashen pale
    (Powder and shot and a scim'tar's gleam).

Teddy has cried, "Let the game proceed!"
    (Powder and shot and a sick'ning shriek),
They quarrel as to which shall do the deed,
And they quarrel as to which shall draw the bead
On the quivering beast and make him bleed
    (Powder and shot and a ruby streak).

Teddy has won by the cast of the dice
    (Powder and shot and a fevered yell),
He has taken aim and his gun speaks twice,
He has taken aim and his gun speaks thrice,
And the tiger has flown to paradise
    (Powder and shot and a dismal knell).

Teddy and Ike are a fearsome pair
    (Powder and shot and a ruby flood),
Stalking the prey to its mountain lair,
Speedy its lope and erect its hair,
Weepful its visage with blank despair
    (Powder and shot and a sea of blood),
    Blood, blood, blood, blood,
    (Blood, blood),
    Blood!

THE PANTOUM OF CONGRESS

[NOTE—For the benefit of the curious it may be explained that the pantoum is a verse form originated by the Malays. Except that it is almost as difficult to construct as it is to read, it has no merit worthy of the attention of the patient reader. It is here used because no occidental verse form could do justice to the subject.]

Gabble and prattle and spiel
    (Congress is at it again);
Six hundred voices a-peal—
    Hark to the tuneful refrain!

Congress is at it again
    (Talk, says the adage, is cheap);
Hark to the tuneful refrain!
    Millions of listeners weep.

Talk, says the adage, is cheap
    (Five thousand shekels a year);
Millions of listeners weep—
    Doomed, by ill fortune, to hear.

Five thousand shekels a year
    (Mileage and perquisites, too);
Doomed, by ill fortune, to hear—
    What can the listeners do?

Mileage and perquisites, too,
    (Gifted with girth is the bill!)
What can the listeners do?
    Hark to the eloquence mill!

Gifted with girth is the bill
    (Twelve hundred hands in the pie!)
Hark to the eloquence mill—
    Hark to the chorusing cry!

Twelve hundred hands in the pie
    (Six hundred voices a-peal);
Hark to the chorusing cry—
    Gabble and prattle and spiel!

To Mrs. Nation

    O val'rous nymph!
        Lion-hearted, Boxer-armed;
O modern counterpart of Joan of Arc,
    With quaking knees
        The beermen flee alarmed
When rumor whispereth that thou'rt on a lark.

    O muscled girl!
        With hatchet in thy hand
(Thy foemen say thou hast a hatchet face);
    O sturdy she!
        The masters of the land
Are all a-tremble at thy least grimace.

    O foe of gin!
        And double foe of beer
In rhymes of "ation" poetasters vie
    To praise thee! 'Gad,
        I'm glad thou art not here,
Else I might go for aye and ever dry!

In Vaudeville

In vaudeville the elder jest
Remains the one that's loved the best;
    For 'tis the custom of the stage
    To venerate and honor age
And look upon the old as blest.

Originality's a pest
That artist's labor hard to best—
    Conservatism is the rage
        In vaudeville.

The artist's arms are here expressed:
A slapstick argent as a crest
    (It is an ancient heritage),
A seltzer siphon gules—the wage
Of newness is a lengthy rest
        In vaudeville.

A Slug of Pessimism

Life is a flower that fades and dies,
    And a cloud that rolls away;
Life is a string of truths and lies,
    Much work and a little play;
Life is a race for the topmost round
    And a fight in the dark alone—
And the end of it all is a hole in the ground
    And a scratch on a crumbling stone.

An Ode to Nelson A.

Commander-in-Chief Nelson A. Miles, who has been made a lieutenant general, will design the uniform of his new and exalted rank.—News Item.

I.
Ah!

II.
Hear the multitude!
And hearken to the sound—
The roof-uplifting paean of admiration!

III.
See the glint—
The glint of polished brass!
The gaudy trappings and
The gleaming gold!

IV.
What splendor!
Ah!
What elegance!
What—ah!

V.
Ah!

VI.
Stay! Nels!
Don't lay on beauties with such lavish hand!
Don't put the brilliant peacock on the bum!
Don't steal the splendor of the azure skies!
Don't grab the gaudiness of fevered dreams!
To dazzle us!

VII.
Hold! Nels!
The glint and dazzle make us wink!
The gold! The brass! The sheen!
The glimmering gleam!

VIII.
The while we humbly bring our fond congratulations
Don't kill us with your

IX.
Mural

X.
Decorations!

To G. W.

(February 22, 1901)

When Valley Forge is long forgot
    And Yorktown's faded from the map;
When none but antiquarians wot
    That you were once a warlike chap;
When people know the Delaware
    As but a stream of germs and mud,
And think Luzon a village where
    The Continentals shed their blood;
When all your monuments are down
    And all your ex-valets are dead;
When history says your hair was brown
    And curled in ringlets o'er your head;
When people know no longer who
    Instructed them in being free,
They will remember that 'twas you
    That hatcheted down the cherry tree!

A Sonnet to a Wienerwurst

Cylindricality is grace, and thou,
    The acme of the form cylindrical,
    Art graceful as a springtime madrigal,
Or the fair curves of Dian's snowy brow;
And also, as the few who love thee vow,
    Thou hast the charm that haunts the mystical.
    Besides, thy toothsomeness is capital—
Far greater than ambrosia's, I trow!
O, fairest flower of Hohenzollern-land!
    Thrice blest thou art, with flavor, charm and grace,
Though cavaliers with stigma would thee brand,
    Yet hast thou fed a sturdy, warlike race;
Their dog-like courage maketh them command,
    And thou!—Tut! tut!—what need to hide thy face?

The Ballade of the Rank and File

The journalistic art is grand,
    And grand it is for those that fill
The benches closest to the band
    And highest up the rocky hill,
    But dank it is, and dark and ill
For those that hang upon the roofs
    And shiver in the outer chill—
The chaps that write the local briefs!

For Richard Harding Davis and
    The other princes of the quill
There's scarce a reader in the land
    That hasn't an admiring thrill;
    The kings of journalistic skill,
The lucky journalistic chiefs
    Tread underfoot those in the mill—
The chaps that write the local briefs!

It's beer and skittles to command
    A big slice from the paper's till,
But sad it is to be a-strand,
    With "Smoke up!" on your tailor's bill!
    The brothers of the bitter pill
(Their woes exceed your worst beliefs!)
    Are those whom tasks inglorious kill—
The chaps that write the local briefs!

O public of the helping hand!
    Look kindly on our crushing griefs!
We constitute a joyless band—
    The chaps that write the local briefs!

To Wu Ting Fang, Envoy Extraordinary and Minister Plenipotentiary

I.
O Wu!

II.
O slant-eyed slave of old Confucius!
O worshiper of bughouse wooden gods!
O swallower of epicurean grub!
O marketer of afterdinner puns!
O master of the festive heated ain!
O thrower gay of double-barreled cons!

III.
You gave old Otis such a jar
That now he's wondering where he are
And if he's perpendicular
Or horizontal!

IV.
Wu!

V.
You smiling son of superstition!
You
Are it, by George!

VI.
Ah me! I like you, Wu!

VII.
So here goes!

VIII.

    Wu Ting Fang,
    There's a military clang
In the Oriental patter of your name!
    And the bassdrum bang
    In the words of your harange
Sets the circumambient atmosphere a-flame!

IX.

    Wu Ting Fang,
    You and Li Hung Chang
Are a pair of mighty mystifying chinks!
    To the diplomatic gang
    (If you'll pardon me the slang)
You have handed out a brace of dinky-dinks!

On Phyllis at the Play

Fair Mistress Phyllis, at the play—
    An angel in an opera cloak—
Perceives the villain stalk and slay
    And sees the hero have his day;
And while the actors weep and joke—
    The people of the mimic world—
She wonders if her cloak is furled
    In just the fashionable way.

An angel 'mid the happy throng—
    An angel by the gates ajar—
Adown the heavens gazes long
    To where earth and its people are;
And while she sees them scrap and tiff
    And laugh and shout and tumble dead,
I wonder if she's wondering if
    Her halo's straight upon her head?

Theatrical Alphabet

A is for actor,—alas 'tis a fact,
There are very few actors that know how to act.

B is for box-office—notice the tin
And the consequent girth of the manager=s grin.

C is comedian—funny, no doubt,
Though when he comes on the spectators go out.

D is for dramatist, smiling and sleek
He makes more in a day than I make in a week.

E is for elephant, used as a cage
For the supers that add to the charm of the stage.

F is for foyer, a favorite resort
When the play is by Ibsen or one of that sort.

G is for gallery—its people like killin'
And cheer when the hero dispatches the villain.

H is the hero referred to above.
He is equally handy and slaughter and love.

I is for ingenue, blithesome and gay.
In the bald-headed row she's the hit of the play.

J is for juvenile—entered her prime
When the drama was back in Solomon's time.

K is the kicker, that croaked 'cause he sat
In a seat to the rear of a theatre hat.

L is for Lylyan, the queen of the "bunch,"
The lobsters provide her with lobsters for lunch.

M is for manager, boss of the play.
He considers the public legitimate prey.

N is for negro,—the minstrel show sort,
His anecdote fund is distressingly short.

O is for orchestra, a la tin-pan-o,
It often consists of a lone, lorn piano.

P is for press-agent, had working cuss.
He invents divorce rumors to entertain us.

Q is for quickly, the way that Macbeth
Retires from the stage when to stay would mean death.

R is the row where the bald-headed gents
Buy $2 seats, disregarding expense.

S is for slapstick, a useful device
For giving a jest the advantage of spice.

T is for Terpsichore, queen of the dance,
And here you perceive how her devotees prance.

U is uncivilized,—such are the jays
In towns where the Uncle Tom's Cabin show plays.

V is for villain, besprinkled with gore
That=s what he is paid every Saturday for.

W is for whiskers,—comedians' are green
Or other quaint colors not commonly seen.

X is the wallet of ten dollar notes
The possession of which crowded houses denotes.

Y is the yokel that comes to the show
Expecting to dazzle the girls of the co.

Z is for zero,—unhappy the day
That the manager skipped with the walking gent's pay.

April

At dawn a gay gallant comes to the eaves
    And trills a song unto his lady fair,
And then, above the reach of boyish thieves,
    A building nest sways in the balmy air;
One day a flower upon a window sill
    Puts forth a bud, and as its beauty grows
    The sun—gay prodigal!—with life-light glows,
    The while he reads the doom of storms and snows;
And then—and then—there comes the springtime's thrill!

Dawn

When like a mist the light gleams in the east
    And like a sea enshrouding fog it lifts,
And far above the clouds part company,
    And rays of purple splendor gild the rifts;
The while the sparrows, high among the eaves,
    Awake to sing their carol to the day,
The city sleeps, unheeding, like a child,
    'Till, clang! the milkman sounds the reveille!

A Villanelle

Another month and then—the spring!
    Hail, happy time of cheer!
When roses bloom and robins sing!

With lift of larks the meadows ring
    And signs of bock beer reappear—
Another month, and then—the spring!

Black mud besmirches everything,
    And gone is winter, sere and drear,
When roses bloom and robins sing.

The wrens resume their chorusing
    And cries of "strawb'r'y" strike the ear.
Another month, and then—the spring.

Our overcoats away we fling
    And grip elixirs disappear,
When roses bloom and robins sing.

The hard and soft coal dealers wring
    Their hands and shed a scalding tear.
Another month, and then—the spring,
When roses bloom and robins sing.

The Transport Gen'ral Ferguson

The transport Gen'ral Ferguson, she left the Golden Gate,
With a thousand rookies sweatin' in her hold;
    An' the sergeants drove an' drilled them, an' the sun it nearly
        killed them,—
Till they learned to do whatever they were told.

The transport Gen'ral Ferguson, she lay at Honolu',
An' the rookies went ashore an' roughed the town,
    So the sergeants they corralled them, and with butt and barrel
        quelled them,—
An' they limped aboard an' set to fryin' brown.

The transport Gen'ral Ferguson, she steamed to-ward the south,
And the rookies sweated morning, noon and night;
    'Till the lookout sighted land, and they cheered each grain o'
        sand,—
For their blood was boilin' over for a fight.

The transport Gen'ral Ferguson, she tied up at the dock,
An' each rookie lugged his gun an' kit ashore,
    An' a train it come and took 'em where the tropic sun could
        cook 'em,—
An' the sergeants they could talk to them of war.

The transport Gen'ral Ferguson, she had her bottom scraped,
For the first part of her labor it was done,
    An' the rookies chased the Tagals and the Tagals they escaped,—
An' the rookies set and sweated in the sun.

The transport Gen'ral Ferguson, she loafed around awhile,
An' the rookies they was soldier boys by now,
    For it don't take long to teach 'em—where the Tagal lead can
        reach 'em—
All about the which and why and when and how.

The transport Gen'ral Ferguson, she headed home again,
With a thousand heavy coffins in her hold;
    They were soldered up and stenciled, they were numbered and
        blue penciled,—
And the rookies lay inside 'em stiff and cold.

    The transport Gen'ral Ferguson, she reached the Golden Gate,
An' the derrick dumped her cargo on the shore;
    In a pyramid they piled it—and her manifest they filed it,
In a pigeon-hole with half a hundred more.

    The transport Gen'ral Ferguson, she travels up and down,
A-haulin' rookies to and from the war;
    Outward-bound they sweat in Kharki; homeward bound they
        come in lead
And they wonder what they've got to do it for.

    The transport General Ferguson, she's owned by Uncle Sam,
An' maybe Uncle Sam could tell 'em why,
    But he don't—and so he takes 'em out to fight, and sweat, and
        swear,
An' brings them home for plantin' when they die.

Faith

    The Gawd that guided Moses
Acrost the desert sand,
    The Gawd that unter Joner
Put out a helping hand,
      The Gawd that saved these famous men
        From death on land an' sea,
      Can spare a minute now an' then
        To take a peep at you an' me.

    The Gawd of Ol' Man Adam
An' Father Abraham,
    Of Joshua an' Isaiah,
Of lion an' of lamb,
      Of kings, an' queens, an' potentates,
        An' chaps of pedigree,
      Wont put a bar acrost the Gate
        When Gabr'el toots fer you an' me.

    The Gawd that made the ocean
An' painted up the sky,
    The Gawd that sets us livin'
An' takes us when we die,
      Is just the same to ev'ry man,
        Of high or low degree,
      An' no one's better treated than
        Poor little you and little me.

THE SPANISH MAIN

Between the tangle of the palms,
    There gleaming, like a star-strewn plain,
All smiling, lies the sea of calms,
    And calls to us to fare amain;
And calls us, as with smile and gem,
    She called that bold, upstanding brood,
Whose bones, when she had done with them,
    Upon her shores she strewed.

Between the tangle of the palms,
    By day the gleam is on the swell,
And drifting zephyrs, bearing balms,
    Her tales of joy and riches tell,
And when the winds of night are free
    Long, glimmering ripples wander by
As if the stars were in the sea,
    Instead of in the sky.

And they went forth in ships of war
    Girt up in all foolhardiness,
To take their toll from out her store,
    Beguiled and snared by her caress;
And we go forth in cargo ships
    To wrest her treasures bloodlessly,
And buy the nectar from her lips,
    Our fairy goddess, she!

Where once their galleons blundered by
    Our cargo ships are on their way,
And where their galleons rotting lie,
    Our cargo ships are wrecked today.
For ever, till the world is done,
    And all good merchantmen go down,
And dies the wind, as pales the sun,
    Her smile will mask her frown.

The Rondeau of Riches

If I were rich and had a store
Of gold doubloons and louis d'or—
    A treasure for a pirate crew—
    Then I would spend it all for you—
My heart's delight and conqueror!

About your feet upon the floor,
Ten thousand rubies I would pour—
    Regardless of expense, I'd woo
        If I were rich.

But as I'm not, I can but soar
Mid fancy's heights and ponder o'er
    The things that I would like to do;
    And as I pass them in review
It strikes me that you'd love me more
        If I were rich.

A Ballade of Protest

(To the address of Master Rudyard Kipling, Poetaster)

For long, unjoyed, we've heard you sing
    Of politics and army bills,
Of money-lust and cricketing,
    Of clothes and fear and other things;
    Meanwhile the palm-trees and the hills
Have lacked a bard to voice their lay;
    Poet, ere time your lyre string stills,
Sing us again of Mandalay!

Unsung the East lies glimmering,
    Unsung the palm trees toss their frills,
Unsung the seas their splendors fling,
    The while you prate of laws and tills.
    Each man his destiny fulfills;
Can it be yours to loose and stray;
    In sophist garb to waste your quills?—
Sing us again of Mandalay!

Sing us again in rhymes that ring,
    In Master-Voice that lives and thrills.
Sing us again of wind and wing,
    Of temple bells and jungle thrills;
    And if your Pegasus e'er wills
To lead you down some other way,
    Go bind him in his olden thills—
Sing us again of Mandalay!

Master, regard the plaint we bring,
    And hearken to the prayer we pray.
Lay down your law and sermoning—
    Sing us again of Mandalay!

Preliminary Rebuke

Don't shoot the pianist; he's doing his best.

    Gesundheit! Knockers! have your Fling!
Unto an Anvilfest you're bid;
    It took a Lot of Hammering,
To build Old Cheops' Pyramid!

The Song of the Olden Time

Powder and shot now fight our fights
    And we meet our foes no more,
As face to face our fathers fought
    In the brave old days of yore;
To the thirteen inch and the needle gun,
    To the she-cat four-point-three
We look for help when the war-dogs yelp
    And the foe comes o'er the sea!

Oho! for the days of the olden time,
    When a fight was a fight of men!
When lance broke lance and arm met arm—
    There were no cowards then!
Sing ho! for the fight of the olden time,
    When the muscles swelled in strain,
As the steel found rest in a brave man's breast
    And the axe in a brave man's brain!

The lance-point broke on the armor's steel,
    And the pike crushed helmet through,
And the blood of the vanquished, warm and red,
    Stained the victor's war-steed, too!
A fight was a fight in the olden time—
    Sing ho, for the days bygone!—
And a strong right arm was the luckiest charm,
    When the foe came marching on!

Oho! for the days of the olden time,
    When a fight was a fight of men!
When lance broke lance and arm met arm—
    There were no cowards then!
Sing ho! for the fight of the olden time,
    When the muscles swelled in strain,
As the steel found rest in a brave man's breast
    And the axe in a brave man's brain!

The Ballad of Ships in Harbor

Clatter of sheers and derrick,
    Rattle of box and bale;
The ships of the earth are at their docks,
    Back from the world-round trail;
Back from the wild waste northward,
    Back from the wind and the lea,
Back from the ports of East and West,
    Back from the under sea.

Here is a bark from Rio,
    Back, and away she steals!
Here from her trip is a clipper ship
    That showed the sea her heels:
South to the Gallapagos,
    Down, due South, to the Horn,
And up, by the Windward Passage way,
    On the breath of the balm-winds borne.

There, standing down the channel,
    With a smoke-wake o'er her rail,
Is a ship that goes to Zanzibar
    Along the world-round trail;
Ere seven suns have kissed her
    She may pound on Quioddy Head,
A surf-tossed speck of melting wreck,
    Deep-freighted with her dead.

And see that gaunt Norwegian,
    Greasy, grimy and black:
She sails today for Yeddo Bay;
    Who knows but she comes not back?
And there is a tramp from Bristol,
    And yonder a white-winged Dane—
Oh, a song for the ships that put to sea
    And come not back again!

Clatter of sheers and derricks,
    Rattle of box and bale;
The ships of the earth are home today,
    Tomorrow they shall sail;
Cleared for the dawn and the sunset,
    Cleared for the wind and the lea;
World-round and back by the olden track—
    Playthings of the sea!

The Violet

    As in the first pale flush of coming dawn
We see a promise of the glorious sun,
    So in the violet's misty blue is drawn
A shadowy likeness of the days to be,
        The days of cloudless skies and poesie,
            When Winter's done.

September

    A dash of scarlet in the dark'ning green,
A minor echo in the night-wind's wail,
    And faint and low, the swirling boughs between,
The last, sad carol of the nightingale.

Arabesque

(An English Version of an old Turkish Lyric.)

The tinkling sound of the camel's bell
    Comes softly across the sand,
And the nightingale by the garden well
    Still warbles his saraband,
But the night goes by and the dawn-winds blow
From the glimmering East and the Hills of Snow,
    And I wait, sweetheart, I wait alone,
    For a smile from thee, my own!

Awake! e'er the gong of the muezzin
    Peals forth for another day;
E'er its loveless, barren toil begin
    But a smile from you I pray!
But a smile from your soul-enslaving eyes,—
As brightly dark as the midnight skies,—
    But a smile, I pray! Awake! sweetheart,
    Awake! my own, my own!

The Rhymes of Mistress Dorothy

Roundel—
Bemauled by ev'ry hurrying churl
And deafened by the city's brawl,
    A helm-less craft I helpless swirl
        Adown the street.

With battered hat I trip and sprawl
    And like a toy tee-to-tum swirl,
To end my strugglings with a fall—

    But what care I for knock and whirl?—
Egad! I heed them not at all;
    For here comes Dolly—sweetheart girl—
        Adown the street!

Triolet—
    The light that lies in Dolly's eyes
        Is sun and moon and stare to me;
    It dims the splendor of the skies—
    The light that lies in Dolly's eyes—
    And me-ward shining, testifies
        That Dolly's mine, fore'er to be—
    The light that lies in Dolly's eyes
        Is sun and moon and stars to me!

Roundelay—
Oh, Dolly is my treasury—
    What more of wealth could I desire?
Her lips are rubies set for me,
And there between (sweet property!)
    A string of pearls to smiles conspire;
With Dolly as my treasury,
    What more of wealth could I desire?

And when have men of alchemy
Yet dreamed of gems like those I see
    In Dolly's eyes, as flashing fire,
    They bid the envious world admire?—
Oh, Dolly is my treasury!
    What more of wealth could I desire?

And then her hair!—there cannot be
Such gold beyond the Purple Sea
As this of mine—unpriced and free!
Oh, Dolly is my treasury,
    My sweetheart and my heart's desire!

Roundel

    If love were all and we could cheat
All gods but Cupid of their due,
    Our joy in life would be complete.

    We'd only live that we might woo,
(Instead, as now, that we might eat,)
    And ev'ry lover would be true,—
        If love were all.

    Yet, if we found our bread and meat
In kisses it would please but few,
    Soon life would grow a cloying sweet,
        If love were all.

WITHIN THE CITY GATES

    We can but dream of murmuring rills
    Mad racing down the wooded hills,
Of meadow flowers and balmy days
When robin sings his amorous lays;
    And lost among the city's ways,
    To us it is not given to gaze
In wonder as the morning haze
    Lifts from the sea of daffodils,—
    Of all but those on window-sills
        We can but dream.

Il Penseroso

Love's song is sung in ragtime now
And kisses sweet are syncopated joys,
The tender sign, the melancholy moan,
The soft reproach and yearning up-turned gaze
Have passed into the caves without the gates
And in their place, to serve love's purposes,
Bold profanations from the music halls
Are working overtime.

In days of old the amorous swain would sigh
And say unto his lady love the while
He pressed her to his heaving low-cut vest,
"Dost love me, sweet?" And she, with many a blush,
Would softly answer, "Yes, my cavalier!"
Now to his girl the ragtime lover says,
The while he strums his marked-down mandolin
"Is you ma lady love?" and she, his girl,
Makes answer thus: "Ah is!"

Gadzooks! it makes me sad! I see the doom
Of Cupid, and upon the battered air
I hear a rumor floating. It is this:
That when the boy god shuffles to the grave
'Tis Syncopated Sambo that will get
His job!

* * * * *

Ah, me! What sadness resteth on my soul!

Finis

There was a man that delved in the earth
    For glittering gems and gold,
And whatever lay hidden that seemed of worth
    He carefully seized and sold;
So his days were long and his store was great,
    And ever for more he sighed,
'Till kings bowed down and he ruled in state—
    And after awhile he died.

    Oh, blithesome and shrill the wails resound!
    Oh, gaily his children moan!
        And the end of it all was a hole in the ground
        And a scratch on a crumbling stone.

There was a man that fought for the right,
    And never a friend had he,
'Till after the dark there dawned the light
    And the world could know and see;
Oh, long was the fight and comfortless,
    But great was the fighter's pride,
And a victor he rose from the storm and stress—
    And after awhile he died.

    Oh, great was the fame but newly found
    Of the man that fought alone!
        And the end of it all was a hole in the ground
        And a scratch on a crumbling stone.

There was a man that dreamed a dream,
    And his pen it served his brain;
And great was his art and great his theme
    And long was his laurelled reign;
But after awhile the world forgot
    And his work was pushed aside,
(For to serve and wait is the mortal lot)
    And then, in the end, he died.

H. L. Mencken

Oh! brown on his brow were the bays that bound
And far was his glory flown!
 And the end of it all was a hole in the ground
 And a scratch on a crumbling stone.

WAR

  The day is not far distant when war, like human sacrifice, will be at an end.—Report of the First Peace Congress.

The good king dreamed the dream
And word went out to all,
  Over the sea
  And under the sea,
And the nations heard his call:
"Have you forgot the Son
 Who made Love conqueror?
  Peace is the Lord's,
  Go sheath your swords!
Let us have done with war!"

From the sky-rim came reply,
And the nations called him blest,
  Over the sea
  And under the sea
Answered the East and West:
"We will slay our kind no more,
 Our murderings shall cease;
  We have bent the knee
  To the holy Tree
Whose snow-white flower is Peace!"

So fell the good king's word,
As a drop of soothing balm,
  Over the sea
  And under the sea
There rolled the pealing psalm:
"Praise Him that sent the Son,
 Who died that we might not die;
  We will sweat no more
  In the bonds of war,
Nor hark to the bugle's cry!"

* * * * * * *

Sudden a trumpet call—
Sudden a flag unfurled—
    Under the sea
    And over the sea
The echo shakes the world!
The nations turn to the strife
As the vultures turn to the dead;
    Yea, we are Huns
    When call the guns,
And the snow-white flower is red!

On Passing the Island of San Salvador

(The first land sighted by Columbus)

Low lies the puny ride of glistening sand,
    Flecked, like a long-lost path, with tufts of green,
    Helpless it seems against the waves, and lean—
Yea, like forgotten offal of the land:
Few watchers pace the measure of its strand,
    Few gleaners in its surge-plowed gardens glean;
    Silent it sleeps, the mocking seas between,
That on the Day the world's great chasm spanned.

Yet, where the fretful breakers battle there
    Time was the Dreamer saw the palms and knew
The victor's joy! To him the land was fair,
    And doubly fair to all his weary crew:
So holds it now the charm of all most rare—
    The deathless beauty of a dream come true!

STARTING FOR THE PLAY

Grace, the cab is waiting.
    We are deuced late.
You are never ready.
    Jove! It's after eight.
Darn this beastly collar
    (Buttonhole's immense).
Shines like celluloid—
    Laundries have no sense.
Opera glasses? Have them.
    Wear your heavy wrap.
Well, then, wear the other.
    How those gloves do gap!
Fix them in the carriage.
    Come, dear, never mind.
Don't stop. Stick a pin in.
    There's no fault to find.
Yes, I've kissed the baby.
    Gad! you do look nice!
What's that? O, your flowers?
    They are on the ice.
Try to hurry, dearie.
    Darn it. Pardon me.
You should hold your train up.
    Yes, I have the key.
Jane will guard the silver.
    Everything's all right.
O, Grace, you must hurry.
    Yes, I fixed the light.
Leave the windows open—
    It's not going to rain.
Everlasting fussing
    Goes against the grain.
What? Your powder chamois?
    O, you goosie, don't!

Put it in my pocket???!!!
    No, my dear, I won't.
You look simply stunning.
    What's up now? O, hang!
(At this point the hall door
    Closes with a bang.)

Good-By, Divine Sarah!

Good-by to you, sweet, Sarah, good-by fair one, divine!
'Tis sad that you will come to us no more across the brine;
'Tis sad to part with you, but hold—a tear bedims our eye;
Guh-guh-guh-guh-good-by, Sarah—good-by—boo-boo!—good-by!

If we are not mistaken, if our mem'ry serves us straight,
We bade you sad farewell, Sarah, in 1888;
And every year since then we've dropt a tear and hove a sigh
When called upon to see you go and whisper sad "good-by!"

The sorrow of those yesteryears is for the nonce forgot,
In our great present sorrow of farewells we'd fain say not,
But since you say, sweet Sarah, "I cannot help it," why
We might as well bear up our best and sob a sad "good-by."

When we are dust and o'er our heads our tombs are in decay,
We shall not then say farewell as we sleep the hours away,
But don't you care, sweet Sarah, if our voices silent lie,
Our children's children will be here to bid you fond good-by.

The Old Trails

As a bird that wandereth from her nest, so is a man that wandereth from his place.—Proverbs, xxvii, 8.

    Let us seek the old trails,
      That led us years agone:
Rambling from the little hills to where we saw the sea;
      Steep they were and bold trails,
      And gleaming in the dawn,
And there, behind their furthest bend, was Home to you and me.

    When we left the old trails
      The world was all before:
Coasts that lured and promised us and stars that showed the way;
      All the roads were gold trails,
      And ev'ry shimmering shore
Called us—scarlet, wanton-eyed!—and who could disobey?

    Now we seek the old trails,
      Searching where they run:
Grass and weeds have swallowed them, and brick and stone in turn;
      Lost they are and cold trails;
      Time and wreck have won!
When the years have shut the book—then, at last, we learn!

The Ballade of Cockaigne

For me the street of pure delight,
    At morn, when like a thief, the day
Steals warily upon the night
    And drives its garish hosts away;
For me the highway ever gay
    Whereon the town's wild children ply,
At dawn to sleep, at night to play—
    On Broadway let me live and die!

For me its endless charms invite,
    Alike when skies are blue or gray,
For me its lamps of red and white
    Ne'er fail to cast a joyous ray;
I would not have my footsteps stray
    Where never sounds its noisy cry;
A fig for every other way—
    On Broadway let me live and die!

Where runs a highroad half so bright?
    Where rises such a soothing bray?
Ah, cheerless is the sorry plight
    Of him who needs must elsewhere stay!
And so I sing my roundelay,
    Old Broadway's name to glorify,
The while a single prayer I pray—
    On Broadway let me live and die!

Street of wild sound and flaming light,
    Though bloodless boobs your charms deny,
Thus sings your humblest satellite—
    On Broadway let me live and die!

Song

Love toils among the reapers
    And wanders in the town;
Love knows no roof to shelter him,
    Nor couch to lie him down.

Love walks upon the waters,
    And fares into the hills;
Love makes himself a hiding-place
    Among the daffodils.

Ah, Love, what lane so winding,
    Ah, Love, what road so long,
That down its path you come not
    With your laughter and your song?

Invocation

God give us strength! We ask no other gift
    Than this alone, the one gift over all;
God give us strength to batter down, to lift,
    To fight, to lose, to raise us from the fall:
        God give us strength!

Strength for the battle, strength to bleed and die,
    Strength for the rout that naught of glory sees,
Strength for Thy service, strength to meet Thine eye,
    Strength to resist the small iniquities;
Strength that, in sinning, we may sin like men,
    Red-blooded sins deserving of the Fire,
Strength that, defeated, we may fight again,
    Strength to make conquest of our heart's desire;
Strength that in all the drudgeries of life
    The joy of effort with us may abide;
Joy in our burdens, joy in love, in strife,
    Joy in our might, our gentleness, our pride!

God give us strength, the one gift over all,
    Leading the worn brigades of Thine own men;
God give us strength, that when we hear Thy call
    Our answer may be: Ready, Lord. Amen.

The Voices

God made men in His image and He gave them of His speech,
    (The gentle voice wind-whispered and the angry thunder roll)
That all may make their prayers to Him, and each may speak to each;
    And love may pass from heart to heart and hate from soul to soul.

So men have learned the speech of Him and hold it for their own,
    (Full many are the voices that He taught them at His knee),
And psalms shall rise forever to exalt Him on His throne:
    Glad anthems of thanksgiving and laments in agony.

The silent voice of stone and scroll, of testament and tome,
    (The centuries hear its echo when its maker's lust is air!)
The voice that roused old Carthage, lifted Athens, conquered Rome,
    That struck the tyrant from his throne and put the cowherd there;

The voice that steals the depths along, the ghostly weeds between,
    (And over the hill and valley, like a flash of glory speeds),
The lowly voice of dot and dash that startles pope and queen—
    Oh, swift it bears its story and a million cars it feeds;

The voice of pike and pennant, of the ensign and the plume,
    (Where yet have men of women born refused to heed its call?)
Of flashing, gaudy panoply, of reds that strike the gloom,
    Like music of a thousand drums it holds the world in thrall;

The voice of powder, shot and steel, of crash and clash and blow,
    (Oh, puny seem the lesser tongues to this of fighting man!)
Of big guns double-shotted hurling thunder at the foe,
    Of needle guns in chorus working out the Father's plan;

And over all, and greatest far, the fateful voice of steam,
    (Grim, certain, deep, immodulate, its whisper gives command),
Yea, go among the busy docks when donkey engines scream,
    And hearken to the Master Voice that fetters sea and land;

Loud sounds it when the dynamos cry shrilly at their bonds,
    (Oh, louder, louder, louder, that the universe may know!)
Loud sounds it when the shafting to the straining crank responds,
    And cross-heads rattle in the slides and tumult reigns below;

Loud pounds its crashing harmony o'er valley, hill and plain,
    (Oh, land and sea are all as one when boilers glow and gleam!)
In foundry, mill and battleship the safety-valves complain,
    And king of all the voices is the croaking voice of steam.

God made men in His image and He gave them of His speech,
    (Oh, many are the voices, but the One is all supreme!)
Shrill echoes of the Master Voice to all the sky-rim reach:
    Hail, Heaven and Earth and Lesser Worlds, the god-like voice of steam!

Appendix

A Kruger

By Edmond Rostand

Mais maintenant, Vieillard, les rois doivent attendre:
    Ne fais pas attendre les rois.
Pour être bien recu comment vas-tu t'y prendre?
    Oh! si tu crains les accueils froids

Pars pour le doux pays des Bibles et des pipes;
    Ses fils ressemblent à tes fils;
Pars pour le doux pays de brume ou les tulipes
    Ont pour petite reine un Lys!

Les rois ne pourront pas vous refuser leur porte;
    Vous entrerez dans leurs palais.
Elle, elle parlera. Faible, elle sera forte.
    Toi, ne dis rien: regarde-les.

Je dis qui l'Empereur aux moustaches en pointes
    Sourira quand cet être clair
Paraitra sur le seuil en disant, les mains jointes:
    "Mon cousin, c'est Monsieur Kruger."

Mais si la Reine echoe—hélas!—tout est possible!—
    Et si toi, vieillard malheureux,
Tu ne rapportes rien que sur la grosse Bible
    Un larme de ses yeux bleus!

Ayant sur ton chemin vu trop de laides choses,
    Apercu trop de coeurs pourris,
Si tu reviens avec des paupières plus closes,
    Des regards plus endoloris.

J'espère, à ton retour, qu'après ce long martyre
    Tu declineras les clameurs;
Tu ne permettras pas que l'Europe s'en tire
    Avec quelques gerbes de fleurs!

Tu diras, en rendant aux fillettes, je pense
    Les gros bouquets aux noeuds flambants:
"Je n'étais pas venu demander à la France
    Des mots ecrits sur des rubans."

Je compte que ton poing fermera la fenêtre,
    Que si la foule crie en bas
Pour s'amuser encore à te faire paraitre,
    Kruger, tu ne paraitras pas!

NOTES

Abbreviations:

BEH   Baltimore Evening Herald
BMH   Baltimore Morning Herald
BSH   Baltimore Sunday Herald
VV   Ventures into Verse (1903)

Adlai. *BSH* (18 November 1900): 4 (in "Knocks and Jollies"). A poem about Adlai Stevenson (1835–1914), U.S. representative from Illinois (1875–77, 1879–81), vice president in the second Grover Cleveland administration (1893–97), and vice-presidential nominee for the Democratic party in the presidential election of 1900 (see note on "One Man Band"). In l. 8, HLM errs in referring to Stevenson as a Hoosier (i.e., a native of Indiana).

And Now Comes Congress. *BSH* (25 November 1900): 4 (in "Knocks and Jollies"). A satirical jab at the incoming Congress (57th Congress, 1901–03).

An Ante-Christmas Rondeau. *BSH* (28 October 1900): 4 (in "Rhyme and Reason"). *VV*. It is unclear whether the epigraph is actually from Marie Corelli, or merely a characterization of her work. Corelli (pseud. of Mary Mackay, 1855–1924) was an immensely popular British novelist whose work HLM repeatedly condemned and lampooned in reviews for conventionality and sentimentality.

April. *BMH* (1 April 1901): 4 (in "Terse and Terrible Texts"; untitled). *VV*.

Arabesque. *VV*.

Auroral. *New England Magazine* 22, no. 3 (May 1900): 275. *BSH* (6 January 1901): 4 (in "Knocks and Jollies"; first stanza only). *VV*.

A Bacteriological Romance. *BSH* (25 November 1900): 4 (in "Knocks and Jollies").

A Ballad of Fierce Fighters. *BSH* (3 February 1901): 4 (in "Knocks and Jollies"). Another poem about the Persian minister to the United States (see note on "To IsaackhanMofakhammetDovlet"). Here the minister is compared to Theodore ("Teddy") Roosevelt, especially in regard to their enthusiasm for hunting.

A Ballad of Impecuniosity. *BSH* (4 November 1900): 4 (in "Rhyme and Reason"). One of many works by HLM on political graft, or influence-peddling.

A Ballad of Looking. *BSH* (25 November 1900): 4 (in "Knocks and Jollies"). *VV*.

The Ballad of Ships in Harbor. *VV*. *Smart Set* 45, no. 3 (March 1915): 226 (unsigned).

The Ballade of Cockaigne. *Smart Set* 44, no. 3 (November 1914): 29 (as by "Herbert Winslow Archer"). See note on "The Old Trails."

A Ballade of Protest. *Bookman* 15, no. 2 (April 1902): 140. *VV*. A poem addressed to Rudyard Kipling (see note on "To R. K."). HLM complains that Kipling has diverted his creative vision from such poems as "Mandalay" (1890; in *Barrack-Room Ballads*), a celebrated poem dealing with the cultural struggle of East and West, and is focusing instead on political and social issues.

The Ballade of the Rank and File. *BSH* (17 February 1901): 4 (in "Knocks and Jollies"). A lament to those humble journalists who write "local briefs" (brief snippets of local news); HLM was one of these for much of his tenure at the *Herald* (1899–1906). In l. 9, HLM refers to Richard Harding Davis (1864–1916), American journalist and novelist who became a celebrated war correspondent during the Spanish-American War and the Boer War.

The Boy and the Man (A Christmas Ballad). *BSH* (23 December 1900): 35. The poem appeared on a full page of the paper, with two large illustrations. It is another treatment of the Filipino war (see note on "The Four-Foot Filipino").

Canzonette. *BSH* (28 October 1900): 4 (in "Rhyme and Reason").

Chrysanthemum. *BSH* (28 October 1900): 4 (in "Rhyme and Reason").

The Coming of Winter. *BSH* (16 December 1900): 4 (in "Knocks and Jollies"). *VV*.

Dawn. *BSH* (27 May 1901): 4 (in "Baltimore and the Rest of the World").

The Dawn of Love. *BSH* (4 November 1900): 4 (in "Rhyme and Reason").

A Dirge. *BSH* (18 November 1900): 4 (in "Knocks and Jollies"). A poem poking fun at the Democrat William Jennings Bryan, losing candidate in the presidential election of 1900 (see note on "One Man Band").

The Donation Party. *BSH* (23 December 1900): 4 (in "Knocks and Jollies").

Faith. *BSH* (9 February 1902): 6 (in "Baltimore and the Rest of the World"). *VV*.

A Few Lines. *BSH* (28 October 1900): 4 (in "Rhyme and Reason"). *VV*.

Fidelis ad Urnum. *BSH* (4 November 1900): 4 (in "Rhyme and Reason"). The title is Latin for "faithful to the urn [i.e., the grave]." "Urnum" is erroneous Latin for "urnam."

The Filipino Maiden. *BSH* (18 November 1900): 4 (in "Knocks and Jollies"). *VV*. In *BSH*, the poem includes a subtitle: "A Ballad of the Trenches." It was presumably omitted in *VV* because "The Four-Foot Filipino" featured the same subtitle.

Finis. *VV*. The poem (whose title is Latin for "the end") is in fact the final poem in *VV*, but it also suggests that the achievements of human life come down, in the end, to a crumbling headstone. The last line of the recurring refrain echoes the last line of "A Slug of Pessimism."

The Four-Foot Filipino: A Ballad of the Trenches. *Leslie's Illustrated Weekly* 90 (6 January 1900): 18. HLM's first poem relating to the aftermath of the Spanish-American War (1898), specifically the battle over the Philippines. The United States annexed the Philippines in 1899, but were then confronted with a native uprising led by Emilio Aguinaldo (who had assisted the United States in its battle to wrest the Philippines away from Spain), and the rebellion was not put down until 1902, after hundreds of thousands of Filipinos had been killed. In ll. 1–3 reference is made to Native American tribes subdued by the United States (Apaches, Osages, Utes, and Sioux). In l. 9, HLM alludes to the Maxim gun, the first self-powered machine gun, invented by Sir Hiram Maxim in 1884.

A Frivolous Rondeau. *BSH* (28 October 1900): 4 (in "Rhyme and Reason"). *VV*.

Good-By, Divine Sarah! *BSH* (17 December 1905): 18 (in "Mere Opinion"). The poem was written toward the end of what was advertised as the final American tour of the French actress Sarah Bernhardt (1844–1923). She gave three performances in Baltimore in December 1905. In fact, she returned to America in 1915.

Il Penseroso. *VV*. The title echoes the second of Milton's pair of poems, "L'Allegro" and "Il Penseroso," which respectively treat the cheerful and the melancholy aspects of life. HLM's poem laments the passing of old-time romance in the modern age.

Im Hinterland. *BSH* (20 January 1901): 4 (in "Knocks and Jollies"). Another poem about the Boer War (see note on "To O. P. K.").

In Eating Soup. *BSH* (20 January 1901): 4 (in "Knocks and Jollies"). *VV*.

In Vaudeville. *BSH* (10 February 1901): 4 (in "Knocks and Jollies"; as "The Rondeau of Vaudeville"). *VV*. For HLM's interest in vaudeville, see note on "The Song of the Slapstick."

Invocation. *Smart Set* 45, no. 3 (March 1915): 211 (as by "James Wharton").

Joe and Bobs. *Leslie's Illustrated Weekly* 90 (31 March 1900): 250. Presumably another poem on the Filipino conflict (see "The Four-Foot Filipino").

Love and the Rose. *BSH* (9 December 1900): 4 (as "Triolets"; in "Knocks and Jollies"). *VV*. In *BSH* the poem is placed under the heading "Imitations—III. Dobson." The reference is to British poet Austin Dobson (1840–1921), who specialized in the writing of triolets.

Madrigal. *BSH* (9 December 1900): 4 (in "Knocks and Jollies"). *VV*. In *BSH* the poem is placed under the heading "Imitations—II. Herrick." The reference is to British poet Robert Herrick (1591–1674), known for his love songs and the musical quality of his verse.

A Madrigal. *BSH* (11 November 1900): 4 (in "Rhyme and Reason"). *VV*. In l. 14, "bar'l" refers to a quantity of money used for political bribery.

The Man That Guards the Grub. *BSH* (25 November 1900): 4 (in "Knocks and Jollies"). In *BSH* the poem is no. II. of "Ballads of the Trenches" (following "The Filipino Maiden"). In ll. 27–28, the reference is to William Tecumseh Sherman (1820–1891), the Civil War general who stated: "War is hell."

Nocturne. *BSH* (11 November 1900): 4 (in "Rhyme and Reason"). *VV*.

An Ode to a "Stein." *BSH* (11 November 1900): 4 (in "Rhyme and Reason"). One of many HLM works praising beer.

An Ode to Nelson A. *BSH* (10 February 1901): 4 (in "Knocks and Jollies"). A poem on Nelson A. Miles (1839–1925), American military leader who was appointed general in the course of the Civil War and later fought in the Indian wars and the Spanish-American War (when he was Commanding General of the U.S. Army). He was made a lieutenant general in 1900. He retired in 1903.

An Old, Old Story. *BSH* (9 December 1900): 4 (in "Knocks and Jollies").

The Old Trails. *Smart Set* 44, no. 3 (November 1914): 25 (as by "Harriet Morgan"). One of many works that HLM wrote to fill up this issue of the *Smart Set*, whose coeditorship he had just assumed; the supply of material had become seriously depleted during the final stages of the editorship of HLM's predecessor, Willard Huntington Wright.

On Passing the Island of San Salvador. *New England Magazine* 33, no. 2 (October 1905): 133. San Salvador (also called Watling's Island), an island in the eastern Caribbean, is reputed to have been the first land sighted by Columbus on 14 October 1492. HLM may have seen it on his own voyage to Jamaica in the summer of 1900. See his later article, "San Salvador, or Watling's Island," in Arthur W. Robson, *By Rail or Water* (Baltimore: Arthur W. Robson, 1911), pp. 41–42.

On Phyllis at the Play. *BSH* (17 February 1901): 4 (in "Knocks and Jollies").

One Man Band. In Charles P. Cleaveland, ed., *Our Flag Song Book* (Baltimore: H. M. Biden Co., 1900), p. [3]. In *McKinley and Roosevelt: Ratification Meeting, Music Hall, September 11, 1900* ([Baltimore, 1900]), p. [2]. A poem lampooning the 1900 presidential campaign of the Democrat William Jennings Bryan, who became celebrated for his flamboyant oratory. Bryan lost to the incumbent president, Republican William McKinley. In l. 25, HLM refers to Bryan's settlement in 1887 in Lincoln, Nebraska; he served two terms as U.S. representative from that state (1891–95). In l. 35, "Teddy" refers to McKinley's running mate, vice president Theodore Roosevelt. In l. 38, "Ad" refers to Bryan's running mate, Adlai Stevenson (see note on "Adlai").

The Orf'cer Boy. *BSH* (2 December 1900): 4 (in "Knocks and Jollies"). *VV*. In *BSH* the poem is placed under the heading: "Imitations—I. Kipling." The epigraph refers to Private Terence Mulvaney, a central character in Kipling's *Soldiers Three* (1888) and other works. As an Irishmen, he frequently speaks in Irish dialect. The sentence used as the epigraph appears in the segment of *Soldiers Three* entitled "The Big Drunk Draf'," as does the spelling "orf'cer."

Outside, Old Year! *BSH* (16 December 1900): 4 (in "Knocks and Jollies").

The Pantoum of Congress. *BSH* (3 February 1901): 4 (in "Knocks and Jollies").

A Paradox. *BSH* (2 December 1900): 4 (in "Knocks and Jollies"). *VV*.

A Preliminary Rebuke. *VV*. The prefatory poem in *VV*.

The Rhymes of Mistress Dorothy. *VV*.

The Rondeau of Riches. *BSH* (23 February 1902): 6 (in "Baltimore and the Rest of the World"). *VV*.

A Rondeau of Statesmanship. *BSH* (30 December 1900): 4 (in "Knocks and Jollies"). *VV*.

A Rondeau of Two Hours. *BSH* (18 November 1900): 4 (in "Knocks and Jollies"). *VV*.

The Roorback and the Canard. *BSH* (28 October 1900): 4 (in "Rhyme and Reason"). A "roorback" is a false or slanderous story told for political advantage; a "canard" is a false or deliberately misleading story, although not one told specifically for political purposes.

Roundel. *VV*.

September. *VV*.

Serenade. *BSH* (20 January 1901): 4 (in "Knocks and Jollies"). In *BSH* the poem is placed under the heading "Imitations—IV. Swinburne." The reference is to British poet Algernon Charles Swinburne (1837–1909), known for his frequent use of repetition in verse.

A Slug of Pessimism. *BSH* (10 February 1901): 4 (in "Knocks and Jollies").

The Snow. *BSH* (20 January 1901): 4 (in "Knocks and Jollies"). *VV*.

Song. *Smart Set* 44, no. 3 (November 1914): 46 (as by "Janet Jefferson"). See note on "The Old Trails."

A Song for Autumn. *BSH* (11 November 1900): 4 (in "Rhyme and Reason"). In ll. 10 and 20, HLM has perhaps deliberately misspelled the verb form "prophesying" ("prophecying" is only a noun).

The Song of the Olden Time. *VV*.

The Song of the Slapstick. *BSH* (9 December 1900): 4 (in "Knocks and Jollies"). *VV*. The slapstick was a wooden clublike object used to produce loud sounds in vaudeville acts. HLM reviewed several vaudeville productions in Baltimore in the *Herald* in 1904–05. See also "In Vaudeville."

A Sonnet to a Wienerwurst. *BSH* (17 February 1901): 4 (in "Knocks and Jollies"). Cf. an unsigned editorial ("Let Joy Be Unconfined," *BSH*, 24 September 1905), celebrating the wonders of the Frankfurter sausage.

The Spanish Main. *BSH* (16 February 1902): 6 (in "Baltimore and the Rest of the World"). *VV*.

Starting for the Play. *BSH* (17 December 1905): 18 (in "Mere Opinion").

Thanksgiving Day. *BSH* (18 November 1900): 4 (in "Knocks and Jollies").

Theatrical Alphabet. *BSH* (17 March 1901); (24 March 1901); (31 March 1901); (7 April 1901); (14 April 1901) (unsigned). A series of couplets accompanied by comic illustrations, all poking fun at the theatrical world. Six letters appeared in each of the first four installment; the final two letters appeared in the fifth installment. In l. 23, HLM alludes to Lillian Russell (1860–1922), one of the most celebrated and beautiful actresses of her generation. In l. 42, HLM refers to George L. Aiken's dramatic adaptation of Harriet Beecher Stowe's novel *Uncle Tom's Cabin* (1852). Aiken's play, first produced in 1852, became one of the most widely seen dramas of the nineteenth century.

The Tin-Clads. *National Magazine* 11, no. 6 (March 1900): 649. VV. Another poem dealing with the suppression of the Filipino rebellion following the Spanish-American War (see note on "The Four-Foot Filipino"). In l. 22, "Tagals" refers to one of the most populous groups of Filipinos, dwelling chiefly on the island of Luzon.

To G. W. *BSH* (17 February 1901): 4 (in "Knocks and Jollies"). A poem about George Washington (1732–1799), on the occasion of his birthday. The final two lines refer to the apocryphal tale of the young Washington's admission that he cut down a cherry tree on his property; the story was invented by an earlier biographer, Mason Locke Weems (1756–1825), in the fifth edition of his biography of Washington (1807).

To Isaackhanmofakhammeddovlet. *BSH* (16 December 1900): 4 (in "Knocks and Jollies"). A poem making fun of the name of the new Persian minister to the United States. His name appears to have been Isaac Khan Mofokhamed Dowleh.

To Kruger. *BSH* (30 December 1900): 1. Another poem about Paul Kruger (see note on "To O. P. K."). It is a translation of a French poem by Edmond Rostand (for the text, see Appendix), published in *Figaro* (9 December 1900). In *BSH* the French text and HLM's translation were printed side by side. In *Newspaper Days* (1941) HLM refers to the work: ". . . in December I received the singular honor of being invited by the new managing editor, Carter, to do a poem for the first page. It was not, to be sure, quite original, for it was based upon a French piece lately published by Edmond Rostand, roundly denouncing the Boer leader, Oom Paul Kruger. Carter put Rostand's French poem into English prose, and I turned it into burnign tetrameter, with poor old Oom reduced to a greasespot at the end. It was blowsy stuff, God knows, but Carter professed to like it, and, good or bad, there it glowed and glittered in longer primer italic on page one—a glory that no other American poet, however gifted, has ever achieved, at least to my knowledge" (ch. 4). HLM's translation is, understandably, rather loose.

To Mrs. Nation. *BSH* (3 February 1901): 4 (in "Knocks and Jollies"). A poem addressed to Carry [frequently misspelled Carrie] Nation (1846–1911), American temperance crusader who famously used a hatchet to damage bars and other establishments selling liquor. As a devoted imbiber, HLM was not her greatest supporter.

To O. P. K. *BSH* (25 November 1900): 4 (in "Knocks and Jollies"). A poem addressed to Stephanus Johannes Paulus Kruger (1825–1904), known affectionately as Paul Kruger or Oom Paul ("Uncle Paul"), president of the South African Republic (1883–1900) who embodied the Boer resistance to the English in the Boer War (1899–1902). The poem refers to Kruger's fleeing South Africa in October 1900 on a Dutch warship; he eventually settled in Clarens, Switzerland, where he died. In l. 10, "gazabo" is a slang term for a man or fellow. In l. 13, "Slipp'ry Dick" refers to Slippery Dick (i.e., Henry C. Miller), who confessed to being a criminal (mostly a thief and bank robber) for fifty years (spending thirty of them behind bars) before converting to Christianity in 1900. He died in 1902.

To R. K. *Bookman* 10, no. 4 (December 1899): 337 (as "To Rudyard Kipling"; as by "W. G. L."). *VV*. A poem addressed to Rudyard Kipling (1865–1936), the British poet and fiction writer who was a dominant influence on HLM's early poetry. HLM particularly enjoyed the vigorous ballads, many of them of a military cast, in *Barrack-Room Ballads* (1892).

To Wu Ting Fang, Envoy Extraordinary and Minister Plenipotentiary. *BSH* (17 February 1901): 4 (in "Knocks and Jollies"). A poem addressed to Wu Ting Fang (Wu Tingfang, 1842–1922), Chinese diplomat who was minister to the United States, Spain, and Peru (1896–1902). In 1917 he served briefly as Acting Premier of the Republic of China. In l. 11, HLM refers to General Harrison Gray Otis, who in September 1898 implemented a law banning Chinese immigrants to the Philippines. Throughout 1899 and 1900 Wu protested this measure to secretary of state John Hay and other officials, but ultimately lost his battle to have it overturned. In l. 25, HLM refers to Li Hung Chang (i.e., Li Hongzhang, 1823–1901), distinguished Chinese general who played a major role in ending the Boxer Rebellion. The final word of l. 4 is difficult to read; it is perhaps a typographical error.

The Transport Gen'ral Ferguson. *Life* 37 (20 June 1901): 532. *VV*.

A Villanelle. *BMH* (29 May 1901).

The Violet. *VV*.

The Voices. *Smart Set* 45, no. 3 (March 1915): 248 (as by "W. H. Trimball").

War. *BEH* (29 April 1905): 7 (as by "J. G."). The poem's authorship is confirmed by the existence of a clipping of it in HLM's scrapbooks (Enoch Pratt Free Library). The first International Peace Congress was organized in 1848 by Elihu Burritt.

A War Song. *BSH* (11 November 1900): 4 (in "Rhyme and Reason"). *VV*. A Kiplingesque poem on the grim toll of war.

Well Buried. *BSH* (25 November 1900): 4 (in "Knocks and Jollies"). A poem about Webster Davis (1861–1923), mayor of Kansas City and secretary of the interior (1897–98) under President William McKinley. He was forced to resign after expressing sympathy with the Boers.

When the Pipe Goes Out. *BSH* (18 November 1900): 4 (in "Knocks and Jollies"). *VV*.

Within the City Gates. *VV*.

[Untitled] ("Laugh while you can," the poet said;). *BSH* (28 October 1900): 4 (in "Rhyme and Reason").

[Untitled] (Count him for lucky whom all women scorn;). *BSH* (4 November 1900): 4 (in "Rhyme and Reason"). One of the earliest of HLM's expressions of skepticism regarding love, romance, and the institution of marriage.

[Untitled] (Sweethearts often quarrel upon). *BSH* (4 November 1900): 4 (in "Rhyme and Reason").

INDEX OF TITLES

Adlai	45
And Now Comes Congress	49
An Ante-Christmas Rondeau	29
April	92
Arabesque	107
Auroral	20
Bacteriologal Romance, A	47
Ballad of Fierce Fighters, A	75
Ballad of Impecuniosity, A	34
Ballad of Looking, A	52
Ballad of Ships in Harbor, The	103
Ballade of Cockaigne, The	122
Ballade of Protest, A	100
Ballade of the Rank and File, The	86
Boy and the Man, The	64
Canzonette	27
Chrysanthemum	26
Coming of Winter, The	60
Dawn	93
Dawn of Love, The	30
Dirge, A	46
Donation Party, The	65
Faith	97
Few Lines, A	24
Fidelis ad Urnum	32
Filipino Maiden, The	40
Finis	113
Four-Foot Filipino: A Ballad of the Trenches	16
Frivolous Rondeau, A	23
Good-By, Divine Sarah!	120
Im Hinterland	73
In Eating Soup	71
In Vaudeville	80
Invocation	124
Joe and Bobs	19
Love and the Rose	59

Madrigal	56
Madrigal, A	36
Man That Guards the Grub, The	50
Nocturne	38
Ode to a "Stein," An	39
Ode to Nelson A., An	82
Old, Old Story, An	58
Old Trails, The	121
On Passing the Island of San Salvador	117
On Phyllis at the Play	89
One Man Band	21
Orf'cer Boy, The	54
Outside, Old Year!	61
Pantoum of Congress, The	77
Paradox, A	55
Penseroso, Il	112
Preliminary Rebuke	101
Rhymes of Mistress Dorothy, The	108
Rondeau of Riches, The	99
Rondeau of Statesmanship, A	70
Rondeau of Two Hours, A	42
Roorback and the Canard, The	25
Roundel	110
September	106
Serenade	72
Slug of Pessimism, A	81
Snow, The	74
Song	123
Song for Autumn, A	37
Song of the Olden Time, The	102
Song of the Slapstick, The	57
Sonnet to a Wienerwurst, A	85
Spanish Main, The	98
Starting for the Play	118
Thanksgiving Day	44
Theatrical Alphabet	90
Tin-Clads, The	17
To G. W.	84
To Isaackhanmofakhammeddovlet	62
To Kruger	68
To Mrs. Nation	79

To O. P. K.	48
To R. K.	15
To Wu Ting Fang, Envoy Extraordinary and Minister Plenipotentiary	87
Transport Gen'ral Ferguson, The	95
[Untitled]	28
[Untitled]	31
[Untitled]	33
Villanelle, A	94
Violet, The	105
Voices, The	125
War	115
War Song, A	35
Well Buried	53
When the Pipe Goes Out	43
Within the City Gates	111

INDEX OF FIRST LINES

A chill, damp west wind and a heavy sky,	60
A dash of scarlet in the dark'ning green,	106
A is for actor,—alas 'tis a fact,	90
A lyric verse I'll make for you,	23
A maiden's heart,	43
A song of birds adown a mine's dark galleries,	74
A youthful bacilla, an amorous blade,	47
Ah!	82
Ah! what were all the running brooks	56
Although you scorn me, I'll forget you not—	32
An ecclesiastic's lot,	65
And now comes Congress,	49
Another day comes journeying with the sun,	20
Another month and then—the spring!	94
As in the first pale flush of coming dawn	105
At dawn a gay gallant comes to the eaves	92
Bemauled by ev'ry hurrying churl	108
Between the tangle of the palms,	98
Christmas Eve when the world's before	64
Clatter of sheers and derrick,	103
Count him for lucky whom all women scorn;	31
Cylindricality is grace, and thou,	85
Dan Cupyd drewe hys lyttle bowe,	55
Fair Mistress Phyllis, at the play—	89
Few roses like your cheeks are red,	24
For long, unjoyed, we've heard you sing	100
For me the street of pure delight,	122
From four to six milady fair	42
Gabble and prattle and spiel	77
Gesundheit! Knockers! have your Fling!	101
Girt up in state the kings await	68
God give us strength! We ask no other gift	124
God made men in His image and He gave them of His speech,	125
Good-by to you, sweet, Sarah, good-by fair one, divine!	120
Grace, the cab is waiting.	118
He looked into her eyes, and there he saw	52

Her father we've chased in the jungle,	40
How can I choose but love you,	36
How like a warrior on the battlefield	38
If I were rich and had a store	99
If love were all and we could cheat	110
If you take a certain view	50
Im hinterland, im hinterland,	73
In eating soup, it's always well	71
In golden mists the day comes gloriously	30
In May they met, in bonnie May,	27
In politics it's funny how	70
In vaudeville the elder jest	80
It's up to me—the winds are chill	29
"Laugh while you can," the poet said;	28
Let us give thanks,	44
Let us seek the old trails,	121
Life is a flower that fades and dies,	81
Love toils among the reapers	123
Love's song is sung in ragtime now	112
Low lies the puny ride of glistening sand,	117
Mum is the man of words,	46
Now comes the roorback	25
Now 'e aren't got no whiskers	54
Now when we mourn the rose and mignonette	26
O, fount of joy!	39
O val'rous nymph!	79
O Wu!	87
Oh, the frost is on the pun'kin	37
Old Joe Wheeler and that little feller Bobs—	19
Oom Paul Kruger,	48
Out in the west, in the land of silver,	21
Outside, old year!	61
Powder and shot now fight our fights	102
Prophet of brawn and bravery!	15
Same old Christmas,	58
Sweethearts often quarrel upon	33
Teddy and Ike are a fearsome pair	75
Ten thousand fathoms deep	53
The Gawd that guided Moses	97
The good king dreamed the dream	115
The journalistic art is grand,	86

The stars in the heavens shine down ev'ry night,	72
The thorn lives but to shield the rose;	59
The tinkling sound of the camel's bell	107
The transport Gen'ral Ferguson, she left the Golden Gate,	95
The wounded bird to its blasted nest,	35
Their draft is a foot and a half,	17
There was a man that delved in the earth	113
We can but dream of murmuring rills	111
We have chased the slick Apachy over desert, plain, and hill,	16
Welcome! Isaac!	62
What's become of Adlai?	45
When like a mist the light gleams in the east	93
When Valley Forge is long forgot	84
When you've spent your bottom dollar	34
Why is a hen? (Kerflop!) Haw, haw!	57

www.ingramcontent.com/pod-product-compliance
Lightning Source LLC
Chambersburg PA
CBHW071121090426
42736CB00012B/1971